D0064034

Substance Misuse and Child Care

How to Understand, Assist and Intervene when Drugs Affect Parenting

Edited by
Fiona Harbin and
Michael Murphy

Russell House Publishing

First published in 2000 by:
Russell House Publishing Ltd.
4 St. George's House
Uplyme Road
Lyme Regis
Dorset DT7 3LS

Tel: 01297-443948
Fax: 01297-442722
e-mail: help@russellhouse.co.uk

British Library Cataloguing-in-publication Data:
A catalogue record for this book is available from the British Library.

ISBN: 1-898924-48-1

Typeset by TW Typesetting, Plymouth, Devon
Printed by Bell and Bain, Glasgow

Russell House Publishing

*Is a group of social work, probation, education
and youth and community work practitioners and
academics working in collaboration with a professional
publishing team.
Our aim is to work closely with the field to produce
innovative and valuable materials to help managers,
trainers, practitioners and students.
We are keen to receive feedback on publications and
new ideas for future projects.*

Dedication

This book is dedicated to all children and families
who are affected by substance misuse and
to Cathy for being so proud of her dad

Contents

Acknowledgements

We wish to acknowledge the tremendous support that we have received from members of Bolton Area Child Protection Committee and Bolton Drugs Action Team and the brilliant contribution of Vicki Ritchie who has spent many hours wrestling with the text.

About this book

Welcome to this book in which a variety of authors and practitioners combine together to create a resource that will be relevant to everyone working with children and parents who are affected by serious substance misuse. This publication will be of particular use to all staff and students who work in agencies that address substance misuse, but it will also prove very useful to those staff and students who work within child care and child protection systems. This is a work that seeks to explain the context and impact of substance misuse on children and their parents, but then goes further to outline positive examples of therapeutic work in response to these different contexts. So it is a work that helps us both to understand and then to address the impact of substance misuse on child welfare.

The proceeds from the sale of this work go directly to fund therapeutic work with children and parents who live in the Bolton ACPC area.

This book is made up of a preface, ten chapters and two appendices.

The preface by Keith Hellawell, the Drugs Tsar, sets the national context for our discussion and indicates current government thinking about substance misuse.

Chapter 1, by Michael Murphy and Fiona Harbin, is an introduction both to the area concerned and to the later chapters in the book.

Chapter 2 by Lilias Alison explores the research evidence that indicates why, and in what areas, substance misuse can negatively impact on parenting and child wellbeing.

Chapter 3 by Marc Gilman addresses social exclusion and parental substance misuse and questions some unhelpful perspectives in these two areas.

Chapter 4 by Eva Elliott and Ali Watson outlines what parents who use substance say they need from staff and agencies that seek to deliver services to families, parents and children.

Chapter 5 by Kamlesh Patel addresses the crucial issue of the minimisation of substance problems in minority ethnic communities and the importance of delivering appropriate and accessible substance and family services.

Chapter 6 by Angie Heal uses one particular example of service provision to explore the range of appropriate residential and community based therapeutic services to children and their parents.

Chapter 7 by Faye Macrory and Fiona Harbin concerns the delivery of appropriate ante and post-natal care to women who misuse substances.

Chapter 8 by Fiona Harbin deals with the provision of therapeutic services to children who have been affected by parental substance misuse, using examples of therapeutic groupwork.

Chapter 9 by Pauline Watts outlines the use of solution focused brief therapy, with families with problematic substance use, to try to help them achieve positive change.

Chapter 10 by Michael Murphy and Gary Oulds concerns the crossover between the substance misuse and child care systems. It explores the difficulties in inter-system working and outlines positive possibilities for working together across system boundaries.

Appendix 1 'Facts about drugs' offers a quick guide to understanding individual substances and their effects on the user. The appendix outlines the impact of amphetamines, cocaine and crack cocaine, heroin and other opiates (reproduced with the agreement of ISTD).

Appendix 2 'Facts about child protection systems' offers a quick and simple guide for substance workers to assist in their understanding of child protection systems.

Notes on Contributors

Lilias Alison trained in Newcastle, Sheffield and Leeds. Her current post is Consultant in Community Paediatrics at The Sheffield Childrens Hospital. Her main interest is in child protection, and is the designated doctor for child protection for Sheffield. Her clinical interest in child protection spans all types of child abuse, and particularly neglect. She did a masters thesis on the outcomes of children whose mothers were substance misusers. Together with other members of the local ACPC, she has tried to promote the needs of children of substance misusing parents.

Eva Elliott is a philosophy graduate. Her doctorate at the University of Manchester examined concepts of community in relation to the provision of community care for people using mental health services, and her work on inner city mental health needs at IPHRP continued this interest. She had been involved in a number of other research projects at the Institute and has a particular interest in the ways in which children manage their health care and conceptualise their needs. Eva left IPHRP in August 1999 and is currently a full time mother.

Marc Gilman has worked in the drugs field in a variety of capacities since the early 1980s. From 1985 to 1999 he worked for The Lifeline Project. Mark's main interest is the relationship between drugs research, policy and practice, in particular the relationships between drugs and crime. In recent years the scope has widened to include the impact that drugs and crime lifestyles have on the children who are raised in those environments. This has neatly coincided with the arrival of his daughters; Jennie in June 1998 and Ella in August 1999.

Fiona Harbin has worked in the child protection unit as a senior social worker specialising in substance misuse and child protection for Bolton social services department, since 1996. Prior to this she worked in Wigan, then Bolton, as a child care social worker. In her current role she has a particular interest in developing new services for working with drug using parents and their children. Within this she has developed group and individual interventions for working specifically with children who have experienced parental substance misuse.

Angie Heal worked for Phoenix for over five years, and spent the last three years there as Community Services Manager, managing a number of small community based projects for drug using offenders and drug using parents. She was also involved in the early stages of multi-agency working in the field of substance misuse and child protection in Sheffield. She now works for NACRO's Crime and Social Policy Section as a policy development officer.

Faye Macrory leads the development of good policy and practice in the treatment and support of pregnant drug users between Manchester Drug Service, St Mary's Hospital, other maternity services and Primary Health Care Teams in Manchester. She is jointly employed by Central Manchester Healthcare Trust and the Mental Health Services of Salford NHS Trust. Over the last five years an inter-agency, collaborative support system has been successfully established across the city and linked in with other services that previously worked in isolation.
The service gives advice about pre-conceptual problems, contraception, sexual problems, sexually transmitted diseases and referral for termination of pregnancy. The service also offers easier access to maternity services to women who are HIV positive and to women working as prostitutes.

Michael Murphy has been involved in child care work for over twenty years. He is currently the resource co-ordinator for Bolton ACPC and a member of PIAT (Promotion of Inter-agency Training). He is the author of *Working Together in Child Protection* (Ashgate, 1995) and *The Child Protection Unit* (Avebury, 1996). He is the co-author of *Dealing with Stress* (Macmillan, 1994) and *Meeting the Stress Challenge* (Russell House, 1996).

Gary Oulds has worked with families as a probation officer, a senior social worker and a health service manager. He was a senior social worker and the team leader for the drug service at Bolton for several years. He is now the substance misuse service manager for Bolton and Wigan Community Health Care, with a particular interest in developing collaborative, inter-agency initiatives to address issues to do with substance misuse.

Kamlesh Patel is currently the Director of the Ethnicity and Health Unit, Faculty of Health at the University of Central Lancashire. A social worker by profession, he has worked within a specialist statutory social services drug team, managed a voluntary drugs and mental health agency (day care, residential and outreach services) as well as being a lecturer and researcher. Kamlesh has also acted as a consultant to a number of national organisations and government departments to identify and develop a range of innovative health and social care services particularly for minority ethnic groups with drug and alcohol related issues and mental ill health. Kamlesh was recently awarded an OBE in the Queens Birthday Honours (June 99) 'for services to minority ethnic health issues.'

Ali Watson joined IPHRP in 1996 from the University of Manchester where she worked as a research criminologist. She has been involved in a variety of projects at the Institute, including an assessment of the needs of children with SLDs and challenging behaviour, and the evaluation of a local pilot GP commissioning group. In 1999 she was awarded a fellowship by the NHS to follow up her research interests in the area of drug use and parenting, and has recently left IPHRP to take up a post at the Drug Misuse Research Unit, University of Manchester.

Pauline Watts is a clinical nurse specialist for families, alcohol and substance misuse. She works for the Options, Community Drug and Alcohol Team at Worthing, West Sussex. She has been in post since 1993, initially to engage women into the service. Previous training in family therapy for two years at the Institute of Family Therapy in London, meant that the introduction of systemic work became a natural progression. Further training and supervision with the Brief Therapy Practice along with the rest of the Options team, has meant the use of brief therapy at Options has been in place for the last four years. She now frequently finds herself giving talks, presentations and training on SFBT use in the drug and alcohol field.

Preface

Keith Hellawell

The government is committed to creating a healthy and confident society, increasingly free from the harm caused by the misuse of drugs. Securing the well-being of children by protecting them from all forms of harm and ensuring their developmental needs are responded to appropriately are equally primary aims of government policy.

Recently in the UK there has been increasing concern about the effects of drug using parents on children. There is some evidence of the emotional, behavioural and learning problems experienced by some children of problem substance misusers. There are a number of potential impediments to the child's health and welfare, including poor bonding with parents; poor parenting skills; uncontrolled drug use and poor uptake of professional help. Although some children may be at risk of neglect or abuse from their parents or guardians who have substance misuse problems, it is important to remember that drug use by parents or guardians is not necessarily an indication of abuse or neglect. Drug use per se should never be used as a reason for dividing families.

The policy context

In 1998, the government launched its ten-year strategy, *Tackling Drugs to Build a Better Britain*. Building on the previous government's strategy *Tackling Drugs Together*, the new strategy commits the government to the task of examining best practice in all areas of the drug strategy and sets out four key aims. These are:

- Helping young people resist drug misuse in order to achieve their full potential in society.
- Protect our communities from drug-related anti-social and criminal behaviour.
- Enable people with drug problems to overcome them and live healthy and crime free lives.
- Stifle the availability of illegal drugs on the street.

The government has maintained its commitment to co-ordination of local strategies by Drug Action Teams (DATs) and is engaged in a number of initiatives such as working towards key performance targets, specifically allocated funding and guidance and policy documents.

The Children Act 1989

Under section 17 of the Children Act, the local authority is able to provide services and support to families where a child is considered to be in need. This may be used to provide services such as advice, counselling, home support or family centre placements to drug using parents and their children. Local authorities are also encouraged to work with parents and required to produce Children's Services Plans that take into account health and education for children and families.

In terms of child protection, the local authority is under a duty to safeguard and promote the welfare of children and prevent their ill treatment and neglect. They are under a duty to make enquiries if they suspect a child is suffering or likely to suffer significant harm. At this stage they are likely to convene a child protection case conference to assess risk and decide whether registration is necessary.

Quality Protects

The Quality Protects Programme is about ensuring that the most vulnerable children in our country get the best that society can offer: the care, safety and security that all children deserve. As part of ensuring children's healthy development it is crucial that they are protected from abuse, physical, sexual, and emotional, and neglect. This is of high priority to the government.

Action to improve the protection of children includes:

- Reform of the regulation system, introducing checks on the full range of children's care services, and strengthening safeguards.
- An extensive range of reforms, set out in the government's response to the Children's Safeguards Review, to improve the protection of all children living away from home.
- Stronger systems for preventing unsuitable people from working with children.
- New strengthened government guidance, written following wide consultation, on how services should work together to protect children.

The document *Working Together to Safeguard Children* (DoH, 1999) sets out the arrangements for the co-operation for the protection of children from abuse. It provides detailed guidance for all relevant agencies on child protection procedures and emphasises the importance of agencies working together to help families and children before abuse has taken place. It provides a clear framework for social workers, the police, teachers, health services staff and others to work together and with families.

Area Child Protection Committees

Area Child Protection Committees (ACPCs) provide the local structures for inter-agency co-operation to safeguard children's welfare across England and Wales. They bring together senior representatives from social services departments, the police, probation, medical practitioners, community health workers, education, voluntary agencies and other interested parties and provide a forum for developing, monitoring and reviewing inter-agency child protection policies, practices and training.

Drug using parent: policy guidelines for inter-agency working (1997)

These guidelines were produced by the Local Government Drugs Forum and SCODA in 1997 highlighting good practice for both statutory and non-statutory agencies and demonstrating the importance of working together to provide an effective response for drug using parents and their children.

Since 1993, as a result of the NHS and Community Care Act (1990), social services departments have been given the responsibility for undertaking assessments of need for people misusing drugs and alcohol in their local community, and devising individual care plans. They also have fund holding responsibilities as regards residential rehabilitation placements and a continued care management role with these clients.

Effective interventions

Delivering services to children in need in our communities is a corporate responsibility. Substance misuse can have an impact on parenting capacity and family life can, in some circumstances, escalate into crisis and abuse. In relation to children and families of substance misusers, improvements in outcomes for children in need can only be achieved by close collaboration between agencies working with substance misuse, local ACPCs and social services departments. Effective collaborative work between staff of social services departments, substance misuse agencies and staff of other disciplines and agencies requires a common language to understand the needs of children, share values about what is in children's best interests and a joint commitment to improving the outcomes for children. The *Framework for the Assessment of Children in Need and their Families* (DoH, 2000) provides this. Good joint working practices and understanding at a local level are vital to the success of interventions with substance misusers and their families. The government acknowledges that working in partnership is essential at every level. Social services departments should, in conjunction with local health and drug services, produce and agree policy and practice guidelines on working with parents who are problem drug users. These guidelines should clarify the issues around drug use and child care to ensure that the needs of children and the needs of the parent are accommodated. The aim should be to reduce the harm associated with drug misuse, both for the children in minimising the risks of abuse or neglect, and for the parents in keeping the family together (where appropriate) and in assisting them to gain access to specialist services. The Area Child Protection Committee should agree the policy and practice guidance. Multi-disciplinary training should support the policy, and drug-using parents should be informed about the policy and how it affects them and their family.

This book follows a successful conference in the North West of England in 1999 that brought together contributors, from all disciplines, to share and discuss their different perspectives. It is a book that tries to achieve a balance between assisting us in our understanding of substance misuse and its impact on children, and helping us to realise what responses children and adults in this situation might benefit from. I recommend it to all those working or studying in this field.

1 Background and Current Context of Substance Misuse and Child Care

Michael Murphy and Fiona Harbin

This is a work that concerns itself with the crossover between serious substance misuse, parenting and the care and development of children. But what do we mean by substance misuse and child protection? Both are areas of significant societal concern fraught with definitional difficulties, not least because the judgement about what is and is not misuse and abuse is constantly changing. For the sake of this work our definition of child abuse will be:

> *Child abuse is an interaction that involves the significant mistreatment of the relatively powerless participant (usually the child or young person) by the participant with more power (usually the parent or adult). This interaction will frequently be affected and partly defined by the child's chronological age, legal status, dependency and developmental immaturity. The definition of what is child abuse will change over time and is affected by the perspectives and values that are influential within society.*
> (Murphy, 1996, p11)

The definition of what is abusive will change over time and, in the same way, the definition of what constitutes substance misuse will change in line with changing societal perspectives. For the sake of this work, we will use substance dependence as the key indicator of substance misuse:

> *a compulsion or desire to continue taking a drug, or drugs in order to feel good or avoid feeling bad. The compulsion or desire is usually initiated following previous repeated use of the drug and is difficult to control. When the compulsion is to avoid physical discomfort it is physical dependence; when it is to avoid anxiety or mental distress, or to promote stimulation or pleasure it is known as psychological dependence.*
> (SCODA, 1997)

But why are we offering this work in the year 2001, when the concern about substance misuse has been expressed for decades, and significant concern about child abuse has been in evidence for even longer? The strength and the longevity of both problems have resulted in a substantial literature in each field. Why isn't it sufficient for the concerned practitioner merely to consult this literature? Our response is that this book is very different. It is not just another work about substance misuse or child abuse as separate entities, but it is about the coming together of the two concerns and the impact of one subject area (parental substance misuse) upon the other (child protection). This work draws together two seemingly separate areas of concern and explores what may occur when they meet in the context of the family. The reason that this work is being offered now is that we are only just becoming aware of the crucial interdependence of substance misuse and child well-being.

What this book does not offer is a substantial or separate study about the effects of alcohol misuse on parenting and child care. This is not because we underestimate the impact of alcohol on parenting and child care. Those who underestimate the power of alcohol misuse to disrupt parenting and child care, merely continue the inappropriate acceptance of alcohol misuse that, for years, has plagued child care systems.

Cases involving only alcohol abuse may have no better a prognosis than those involving the abuse of other substances but cultural biases may be more accepting of alcohol abuse. (Murphy et al., 1991, p208)

It is rather that the effects of alcohol have been thoroughly outlined and evaluated in other works (Gordon, 1989; Velleman, 1993; Laybourn et al., 1996; Brisby et al., 1997; Houston et al., 1997) that we have permitted ourselves not to dwell on alcohol as a separate entity. We wish to acknowledge both that alcohol can have a significant negative impact on families and children, and that parents who misuse other drugs will often mix these substances with alcohol (see Chapter 4). When we look at concerns about substance use (see Chapter 2) we see that these often mirror our concerns about alcohol misuse. For the sake of this work, substance misuse means the misuse of illegal substances or prescribed medication, but we acknowledge that this misuse is frequently accompanied and exacerbated by the misuse of alcohol.

It is also the case that this work does not concern itself with recreational use of substances, which probably accounts for the majority of substance use in the country:

Research shows that many people experiment with drugs, with most trying them only once in a life time. Fewer, but a significant minority, use drugs regularly. Around one-third of people who have ever used drugs become regular drug users, and it has been predicted that roughly ten per cent become problem drug users. (SCODA, 1997, p10)

This work is concerned with substance misuse that is dependent or chaotic. For the practitioner and the client, the ability to distinguish recreational use from problematic misuse is a crucial skill.

Assessment

This work does not assume that a substance problem in a parent automatically leads to serious child care or child protection problems:

> *To suggest that all parents who suffer from problem drug use present a danger to their children is misleading. Indeed, much research indicates that in isolation problem drug use of a parent presents little risk of significant harm to children.* (Cleaver et al., 1999, p23).

If substance misuse alone was seen to indicate child care problems, then child protection systems would quickly become swamped with adult substance referrals: '. . . it is important not to generalise, or make assumptions about the impact on a child of parental drug and alcohol misuse. It is, however, important that the implications for the child are properly assessed' (DoH, 1999, p9).

Doing this proper assessment is not as easy as it may seem. Substance use and parenting are both activities that occur in the private domain, outside general public scrutiny. However, practitioners from the substance arena have become adept at making assessments of substance use and child care workers routinely assess parenting. But problems may arise when practitioners are asked to (a) share information with other systems about their assessments (thus breaking single system rules about confidentiality) and (b) make assessments of the impact of one area on the other. Substance practitioners will disclose nervousness about assessing parenting and child care, and child care practitioners frequently confess ignorance about the assessment of substance misuse: 'Child-centred agencies may not understand or feel confident in dealing with drug users, while specialist drug services may not understand the needs of children or child protection procedures' (SCODA, 1997, p4).

The two different assessment processes, that would normally be completed by practitioners in both systems, need to come together in a three stage process that measures both substance misuse and its subsequent impact on the child (Figure 1).

The first stage of the process involves a measurement of substance use that would traditionally have been the job of the substance practitioner. This includes the usual issues. What substances are in use? How are they taken? The quantity of use? When the substance is used? With whom? Is the use recreational, chaotic, or dependent?

It is important to undertake some assessment of the lifestyle implications associated with the procurement of the substance: '. . . finding money for drugs and/or alcohol may reduce the money available to the household to meet basic needs, or may draw families into criminal activities (DoH, 1999, p10).

This stage of the assessment process discovers the place of substance in the life of the parent and their individual relationship to that substance.

Figure 1. The assessment process

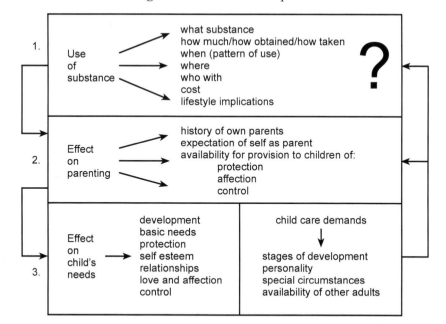

The second stage of the assessment seeks to examine the effect of the substance on the user as a parent. This part of the assessment includes the person's own history of being parented, the expectations of themselves as parents, their parenting patterns when using or reducing use and finally, the effect of substance on parental availability, affection, control and discipline. This part of the assessment examines a parent's capacity with regard to the parenting task (this coincides with *the dimensions of parenting capacity*, 'The Framework for the Assessment of Children in Need' DoH, 2000, p21).

The third part of the assessment has two elements: the first is the effects on the child of the style of parenting outlined in stage two. This part looks at what the child needs from their parent and measures how well the child's basic needs, need for protection, need for stimulation, need for love and affection and need for control are being met (this coincides with *the dimensions of the child's developmental needs* in 'The Framework for the Assessment of Children in Need' DoH, 2000, p19).

The second element is an assessment of the level of child care demand on the concerned parent. Thus the level of demand will go up and down depending on the number, developmental stages and personalities of the children concerned (sickness or disability impacts significantly on this demand). This part also includes a consideration of who is available to share responsibility for this child care demand, including other parents, grandparents, other relatives or significant family friends.

Figure 2. Assessment framework

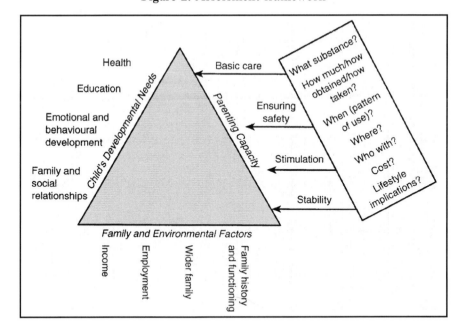

If parental misuse in stage one is combined with a minimal effect in stages two and three, then that situation does not warrant a child care or child protection referral. However, if patterns of use in stage one exaggerate existing problems in stage two, and assessment in stage three indicates high child care demand and significant unmet need, then action will be required from both substance and child care systems.

The assessment process that we suggest is not an alternative to the new *Assessment framework* (DoH, 2000) rather it is an additional element (Fig. 2) that effects all three domains of the assessment triangle. One positive aspect of using the framework is that it encourages us to assess family strengths as well as weaknesses, which is particularly important in substance misusing families where often only negative are seen. In this assessment (Fig. 2) we measure the use of substance as a separate element and then track the effects of this use through the other three domains, parenting capacity, child development and family and environmental factors.

The additional element of substance misuse may exaggerate or highlight several dimensions in each domain of the assessment triangle. So, in our example, in *parenting capacity*, basic care, ensuring safety, stimulation and stability have been singled out for special consideration. In the *child's developmental needs* we have highlighted health, education, EBD and social relationships. In *Family and Environmental factors*, family history and functioning, wider family, employment and income have been brought to the fore. However, in a particular family, with a particular substance or pattern of use, other dimensions of the framework may need special consideration within the assessment.

The crucial dilemma during the assessment process is also the critical concern of this book: what types/levels/complexities of substance misuse, in what kind of family systems, will lead to significant harm or impairment, to which types of children? Conversely, what types of substance misuse, in what kind of family systems, will lead to minimal harm to children? Furthermore what types of professional interventions will help reduce this harmful impact on children?

The assessment process involves the complex interaction between substance use, effect on parenting capacity and child care demand and unmet need. But as well as measuring the impact of substance misuse, it is crucially important to measure other family and environmental factors (DoH, 2000), particularly family disruption and disharmony:

> *. . . there is a considerable body of evidence to suggest that . . . problem drinking or drug use, which is not accompanied by other family stressors, presents fewer risks to the children . . . The impact is also likely to be ameliorated when family life is harmonious and one parent is available to ensure the emotional and physical well being of the children.* (Cleaver et al., 1999, p39)

However, it is also the case that substance misuse (Gordon, 1989) can have a considerable impact on family disharmony: '. . . problem alcohol or drug use can place considerable strain on relationships between spouses or intimate partners. Problem drinking and drug use is associated with domestic violence' (Cleaver et al., 1999, p39).

National and local issues

Nationally, there appears to be very little systematic collation of statistics and trends on the impact of parental problematic drug use on child care and parenting. In 1997 workers from Bolton sent out research questionnaires to all ACPCs in England and Wales. These requested data on the number of children on the child protection register, or in the looked after system, where parental drug use was recognised as a contributory factor. Whilst expecting a limited response, those ACPCs that did return questionnaires were generally unable to provide the information requested. Those ACPCs who were able to provide the relevant information indicated that there was a link between parental drug misuse and issues of neglect and emotional abuse for the families that they were working with. Forrester, (2000) in his Bermondsey sample confirmed that 'substance misuse was strongly related to neglect and cases were twice as likely to be subject to care procedings' (p235). This confirmed the conclusions of the research that we were undertaking in Bolton (see below).

Whilst these figures may reflect increasing worker awareness of drug misuse, an increasing ability to identify when this has become problematic, and a willingness to speak openly with families about drug use, they also reflect the increase in drug misuse in society as a whole.

Dependent drug use escalated in the 1980s, with the increasing availability of heroin from the Middle East, against the social backdrop of the rise in long-term unemployment. The number of new drug users notified to the Home Office in 1985 was 6409, compared to 1600 in 1980 and just 711 in 1970. Research revealed that the majority of the new drug users were from deprived areas with high rates of unemployment and social exclusion (Buchanan and Wyke, 1987). Drug use has continued to expand in the 1990s, with more recent figures indicating an increasing number of women users and a far younger population of drug users as a whole. With the majority of women users being of a childbearing age, it can be assumed that the links between drug use and parenting will continue to increase.

Research from the United States indicates that problematic drug use impacts detrimentally on the willingness of parents to work with agencies following the identification of child concern (Murphy et al., 1991). This, in its turn, makes it less likely that children will remain in the care of their parents or return to their care after a period in the looked after system. These trends are becoming visible in the UK, where the impact of substance misuse on child protection and looked after systems is increasing.

These national issues are reflected strongly in local awareness and local practice. In Bolton, in the late 1980s and early 1990s, child care practitioners began to express great concern at the noticeable rise of substance problems in families with whom they were working. Then in October 1989 a young child was abused and killed in a household where there were serious substance problems. Practitioners and managers were faced with a subsequent dilemma, how could they measure the impact of that parental misuse on the care, development and protection of children? The first recommendation of the case review into the child's death was that a mechanism be found to properly assess drug using families. At this time the substance and child care systems, having travelled on very separate paths, were forced to work more closely together (see Chapter 10). A training course was developed in 1992 both to inform child care workers about substance misuse and substance workers about child protection, and to facilitate the exploration of the crossover between the two worlds. A 'snapshot' of Bolton ACPC's child protection register in 1995 indicated that over 50 per cent of children on the register came from households where substance misuse was a significant issue and an even higher proportion of children in care proceedings were seen to be severely affected by familial substance misuse. Then in 1997 a five-year-old boy was murdered in a drugs related attack. The reaction of the whole community was profound. This was a final, symbolic proof that substance could have a dramatic, negative impact on a child's well-being.

In 1998 a group of staff from the substance and child care systems in Bolton decided to organise a national conference to promote a wider discussion about the crossover of substance misuse and child care. The conference was held on 19/2/1999 in Bolton and was well received, both because of the quality of speakers, and the opportunity the conference gave to staff to share their experience with others working in this field. Two hundred and fifty participants were able to attend the conference, but the concerns they expressed indicated a more substantial demand for information and knowledge in this area. The conference organisers recognised the need for a wider dissemination of that information and so began the process of producing this book.

This book deals with the context of substance misuse and child care, it explores the crossover between the two issues and the two systems, but it does not stop there. To describe a problem without attempting to outline appropriate responses is not useful to practitioners or managers; therefore the book offers a final five chapters on appropriate therapeutic and strategic responses in practice.

References

Brisby, T., Baker, S., and Hedderwick, T. (1997) *Under the Influence: Coping with Parents who Drink too Much*, London: Alcohol Concern.

Cleaver, H., Unell, I., and Aldgate, J. (1999) *Children's Needs–Parenting Capacity*, London: HMSO.

DoH (1999) *Working Together to Safeguard Children: A Guide to Inter-agency Working to Safeguard and Promote the Welfare of Children*, London: HMSO.

DoH (2000) *Framework for the Assessment of Children in Need and Their Families*, London: HMSO.

Forrester, D. (2000) Parental Substance Misuse and Child Protection in a British Sample, *Child Abuse Review*, Vol. 19, 235 – 46.

Gordon, L. (1989) *Heroes of their own Lives: The Politics and History Of Family Violence, Boston 1880–1960*, London: Virago.

Houston, A., Kork, S., and Macleod, M. (1997) *Beyond the Limit: Children who Live with Parental Alcohol Misuse*, London: Childline.

Laybourn, A., Brown, J., and Hill, M. (1996) *Hurting on the Inside:Children's Experiences of Parental Alcohol Misuse*, Aldershot: Avebury.

Murphy, J.M., Jellinek, M., Quinn, D., Smith, G., Poitrast, F., and Goshko, M. (1991) Substance Abuse and Serious Child Mistreatment: Prevalence, Risk and Outcome in a Court Sample, *Child Abuse and Neglect* Vol. 15 no3, 197–211.

Murphy, M. (1996) *The Child Protection Unit*, Aldershot: Avebury.

SCODA (1997) *Drug Using Parents:Policy Guidelines for Inter-agency Working*, London: LGA Publications.

Velleman, R. (1993) *Alcohol and the Family*, Institute of Alcohol Studies.

2 What are the Risks to Children of Parental Substance Misuse?

Lilias Alison

This chapter deals with the central issue of how substance misuse may seriously impact on parenting and the well-being of children. It does not imply that all substance misuse automatically leads to negative consequences, but it presents relevant research material to highlight the possible negative implications of substance misuse on child care.

People who misuse substances are often young, of child bearing age and many have children. Over the last two decades, a significant amount of evidence has accumulated raising concerns about the effects of parent's drug taking on the welfare of children, and in particular linking parental substance misuse with child abuse and neglect.

Black and Mayer (1980) were amongst the first to raise concerns about children of substance misusers. Their study of two hundred families with an alcohol or opiate addicted parent, found that some degree of neglect had occurred in all; physical or sexual abuse had occurred in over one fifth of the families; and serious neglect in around one third. Since then, a number of further (mainly American) studies have shown the risks of child abuse and neglect in children of substance misusers (Jaudes et al., 1995, Wasserman and Leventhal, 1993; Kelley, 1992), and the risks of repeated maltreatment (Wolock and Magura, 1996). Further research has also shown that children of substance misusers have high rates of removal into care (Famularo et al., 1992; Kelley et al., 1991; Kelley, 1992; Regan et al., 1987) with evidence from Europe, USA and the UK suggesting that 30–50 per cent of children ultimately no longer live with their mothers (Baller, 1994; Merrick, 1985; Fraser and Cavanagh, 1991; Regan et al., 1987). There is also clear evidence implicating maternal substance misuse as one of the most significant predisposing risk factors for abused children as a group. Such evidence includes studies of children subject to care proceedings and studies of children in care. For example, in a study of care proceedings undertaken because of abuse, half the parents had misused alcohol and or drugs (Murphy et al., 1991), and another Boston court sample identified that over two thirds of abused children had parents who were classified as drug misusers (Famularo et al., 1992). A study of children in voluntary child welfare agencies in the USA found that over half were affected by familial alcohol or drug abuse (Curtis and McCullough, 1993). The huge increase in requirements for foster care in the USA in the early 1990s was ascribed to rising rates of substance misuse (Kelley, 1992; Curtis and McCullough, 1993), and it would seem likely that similar trends are taking place in the UK. These studies clearly suggest that parental substance misuse and child abuse are closely associated.

All types of abuse have been associated with drug misuse (Merrick, 1985; Famularo et al., 1989; Famularo et al., 1992; Murphy et al., 1991; Wasserman and Leventhal, 1993; Jaudes et al., 1995), with neglect being the commonest problem. Toddlers are especially vulnerable (Jaudes et al., 1995; Wasserman and Leventhal, 1993). Sexual abuse has also been associated with parental drug abuse, for example, in one study of sexually abused girls, over one third had mothers who were drug abusers (Leiffer et al., 1993). Cocaine use too has specifically been associated with child sexual maltreatment (Famularo et al., 1992).

Drug abuse and parenting

There are many reasons why substance misusing parents may not be able to provide good care to children. Firstly, they may enter adult life equipped with poor parenting skills, as they themselves may have been poorly parented. Substance misusing mothers as a group show increased rates of abuse in their own childhood, with in some cases, abuse continuing into adulthood (Black and Mayer, 1980; Tyler et al., 1997; Regan et al., 1987). Drug abuse can provide an escape from negative childhood experiences (Regan et al., 1987; Davis, 1990), which may themselves need addressing before mothers can become effective role models for their children (Davis, 1990). Secondly, the very nature of drug taking could directly affect their child care. Finding the resources for drugs and drug seeking will take time away from child rearing. Being under the influence of and recovering from drug effects, may also influence how a parent can care for a child. This is particularly true if those effects include irritability, paranoia, altered mood, impaired judgement, impulsivity, drowsiness and unconsciousness (Gawin and Ellinwood, 1988; Famularo et al., 1992). Additionally, certain drugs themselves have specific effects which may lead to specific types of abuse, for example alcohol abuse has been linked particularly with physical abuse of children, and cocaine use with child sexual abuse (Famularo et al., 1992). Finally, parent's difficulties may not be limited to those associated directly to their addiction. As a group, substance misusing parents have been found to have increased risks for other emotional difficulties, attentional deficit, psychiatric and mood disorders which impact on their ability to care for children (Kolar et al., 1994; Famularo et al., 1989; Gawin and Ellinwood, 1988). Parenting and attachment may also be significantly disrupted because of repeated separations due to hospitalisation or imprisonment (Kolar et al., 1994).

Child factors and parenting stress

The children of substance misusers who have been exposed to drugs in utero might themselves be more difficult to care for, creating greater parental stress, which in turn may contribute to child abuse. Drug withdrawal in these infants may lead to stiffness, agitation, over activity and restlessness with unpredictable fluctuations in their behavioural responses. These symptoms can persist for several months. In the case of methadone, withdrawal symptoms may be late to develop, intensifying at 2–4 weeks of age (Rothstein and Gould, 1974). These factors make infants difficult to comfort, and interrupt the normal process of attachment (Chasnoff, 1988). Even experienced foster carers are more likely to find these children stressful (Kelley, 1992).

In addition, the effects of early separation from the baby may itself be associated with later parenting difficulties. Drug addiction may increase the risk of premature birth, and other conditions which can require special neonatal care, enhancing the probability of separation (Kelley, 1992; Bays, 1990). Further contributing to parenting stress, is the increased later risk of delayed mental and language development, and poorer social adjustment in the child (van Baar and de Graff, 1994). It may be difficult to unravel whether these risks are related to prenatal drug exposure, or due to environmental factors (Davis, 1990; Soepatmi, 1994; Ornoy, 1996).

Incidence of child abuse in the UK
In considering the outcomes for children of substance misusers, it is important to look at evidence from the UK, as results from elsewhere might not be applicable to UK populations. Most studies of drug misuse and child abuse are from the USA, where there are significant differences both in terms of drug taking habits (crack cocaine rather than heroin being the major problem); ethnicity of drug users; and the legal and social services approach to drug using mothers.

There is remarkably little literature from within the UK documenting child abuse and parental drug misuse. Fraser and Cavanagh (1991) reviewed the outcomes of 94 London drug addicts who had delivered in a London hospital and traced the outcomes of their 108 babies 1–18 years later. Three quarters of the mothers were still addicted, and amongst them, 63 per cent of their children were living apart from their mothers. Of those mothers who had ceased addiction, only 4.5 per cent of the children were living apart from their mothers.

Recently Alison and Wyatt (1999) followed up the outcomes of Sheffield children, whose mothers had identified themselves to the neonatal services as having either taken illicit drugs or methadone during pregnancy. These mothers were compared with a control group of non-drug using mothers who were matched on postal code, and child age. In both groups of mothers, the maternal age, ethnicity, and Townsend scores of deprivation were very similar (Townsend et al., 1988). Amongst the drug taking mothers, patterns of drug use ranged from those with recreational drug use; those who may have ceased drug taking early on in the pregnancy; those who were on a controlled daily methadone dose (ranging from 2–60mg daily); to those who had a severe addiction and poly-drug use. There were highly significant

Table 1. Social services outcomes for drug exposed children and controls

	Drug exposed	
	Controls (a) (n = 48) %	Significance (b) (n = 48) %
Any social services involvement	85.4	6.2***
Enquiry to register (index child/sibling)	10.4	0
Case conference held	52.1	0***
Index child registered	37.5	0***
Fostered at any stage	31.3	0***
Child in care other than mother	35.4	0***
Care proceedings/care orders	37.5	0***
Adopted	6.3	0
Died	2.1	0

(a) Controls matched on date of birth, and postal code.
(b) Significance testing using McNemar test, ***$p < 0.001$.

differences in the child abuse rates and social outcomes between the drug taking mothers and the control group, by the time of the study when the children were aged 18 months–five years (Table 1).

Those children with poor social outcomes were not limited to being the offspring of those severely addicted mothers. There were similar proportions of poor child protection outcomes amongst the children of mothers using prescribed methadone. The reasons for this could not be clearly identified, but factors including changing drug taking habits, or changes in the domestic situation, and new drug using partners, are likely. Those babies experiencing withdrawal symptoms in the newborn period, were most likely to have the poorest social outcomes, presumably because these were babies of mothers who had continued drug taking right up until the birth. There were 75 child protection conferences held for 25 of the children. The majority (80 per cent) of initial child protection conferences were held as a result of an incident or because of concerns about actual neglect, rather than being held as planning conferences around the time of birth (Alison and Wyatt, 1999).

Child neglect

Child neglect is the commonest type of abuse amongst children of substance misusing parents and may encompass many areas including medical neglect, failure to provide adequate food, clothing, accommodation, and protection from injury and harm.

Medical neglect

Medical neglect such as failure to fully immunise and failure to attend routine health surveillance and screening is more common in children of substance misusers (Merrick, 1985; Kelley et al., 1991). Non-attendance at follow up clinics can lead to failure to follow up potential blood borne viral infections such as Hepatitis B and C, resulting in children in the community having uncertain infection status. In children of substance misusing parents, the clinic non-attenders are often those children who are particularly vulnerable and who have greatest morbidity (Chan et al., 1986).

Failure to attend to child health matters may occur through parental neglect, but also because of frequent address moves, including moves into care. These may result in multiple changes in professionals (such as GP, health visitor, school nurse or social worker) who will have incomplete health records or records that are not passed on. Difficulties in tracking children can occur also because of changes of name.

This group of children may also fail to thrive for various reasons. A mother's appetite can be suppressed from drug taking, and she may not respond to her child's need for food. Poverty might contribute, with resources being spent on drugs rather than food (Bays, 1990). Parents oversleeping due to drug effects could result in children missing meals, and catch up growth can occur in care simply as a result of the child receiving three meals a day rather than two. Failure to thrive needs to be adequately assessed, identifying the organic problems such as, severe intrauterine growth retardation and non-organic causes (e.g. lack of food, cooking facilities, parents oversleeping). Consideration needs to be given to the longer term effects of neonatal drug exposure (organic cause) which may impair growth both prenatally and postnatally (Chasnoff et al., 1980).

Developmental delay and education

Professional concerns about developmental and educational progress of children of drug using parents are not uncommon. It may be hard to unravel the extent to which these outcomes are due to prenatal drug effects or to environmental factors. There have been several studies identifying developmental delay in children exposed prenatally to drugs (van Baar and de Graff, 1994; Tyler et al., 1997; Olofsson et al., 1983; Ornoy et al., 1996) although other studies of children exposed only to methadone are much more optimistic (Burns et al., 1996; Wilson, 1989). Specific drug effects can be important with respect to child development. For example, infants of amphetamine users may be very sleepy and unresponsive for several months, before becoming more alert and interested, which would appear to be a direct drug related effect. In children of mothers who may also have misused alcohol in pregnancy, the possibility of foetal alcohol syndrome should be considered, as this may result in developmental delay and specific problems with co-ordination and attention (Larsson et al., 1985).

The home environment plays a very important part in the child's development, and the drug user may not provide a particularly stimulating environment for the child. There is some evidence that substance misusing mothers spend less time in family activities and meaningful play (Bays, 1990). However, there is also evidence that mothers previously addicted to heroin, and who enter methadone treatment, spend more time with their family once they are in treatment (Reno and Aiken, 1993). It would be expected that if environmental factors are affecting the child's development, then the child would show improvements in foster care. However, the evidence in favour of this is difficult to interpret. Tyler et al. (1997) examined development scores between two groups of children aged six months, half of whom had been placed in family foster care, the other half had stayed with their mothers. The developmental scores of those children still with their mothers were better, although there was a higher death rate in this group. The poor outcomes of those in foster care might be related to the quality of foster care in this series, as some of the foster carers were grandmothers who had other children to care for, and had many other stresses in their lives. In addition, testing infants at six months can be too early to reflect the influences of the carer, and it may therefore be more valid to examine for environmental factors later in the child's development at around 18 months. Comparing the developmental progress of children of drug users to those children whose parents are not drug users shows that there is divergence in development from 18–24 months. This is the case with early language (18–24 months), and becomes particularly significant in children by the age of five years. These effects appear to be environmentally induced, since a fostered subgroup of children from the drug using parents showed catch-up development (van Baar and de Graff, 1994). Ornoy (1996) carried out a further study of children of heroin dependent mothers and compared developmental outcomes of children raised at home to a group who were adopted at a very young age. All these children were compared to a control group of children from non-addicted parents. Those adopted early functioned similarly to the controls and had normal development, whereas those raised at home had lower IQs and higher incidence of hyperactivity, inattention, and behavioural problems (Ornoy et al., 1996). Other studies of older children have also recognised concerns about developmental progress in school, and that behavioural difficulties and truancy are more common (Kolar et al., 1994). Comprehensive intervention programmes for parents may have a significant positive effect on improving child development (Jansson et al., 1996).

Accidents and injuries
Even where parents supervise children perfectly adequately, accidents happen to children. In children of drug users, there can be an excess of preventable accidents or accidents occurring because of a lack of supervision. In the Sheffield study, the children of drug using mothers presented with a similar frequency to hospital for accidents and emergencies, compared to the children of non-drug using mothers, but the problems being presented to hospital were qualitatively worse, raising concerns about possible non-presentation of more minor injuries.

Accidental poisoning or drug ingestion are common childhood problems, usually occurring if these substances are left out and the carer is briefly distracted. The scope to ingest drugs could be greater for children of substance users because drugs may be present in the home and be accessible, and because of poor levels of supervision. Some of the commonly used drugs such as methadone and cocaine are extremely dangerous to children (Bays, 1990; Binchy et al., 1994; Rivkin and Gilmore, 1989). Drugs can also be deliberately administered to children in order to keep them quiet, or to make them sleep (Schwartz et al., 1986). Parents need to be advised about safe storage of drugs, and the risks posed by exposure of children to illicit drugs.

Case example
Joe, aged 11 months, was first seen in the local accident and emergency department after ingesting dettol. He was seen in a second accident and emergency department at 33 months after ingesting temezepam (benzodiazepine) in a sufficient quantity to warrant a stomach washout and admission. He was again seen back at the first accident and emergency department at 34 months after again ingesting temezepam. On this occasion his mother had treated him with salt hoping to induce vomiting at home (a very dangerous manoeuvre in a young child). He was later placed on the child protection register under the category of neglect.

Case example
Jamie, aged 24 months, presented to the accident and emergency department after apparently accidentally ingesting two spoons of methadone. She was extremely drowsy, with pinpoint pupils, and required admission to intensive care and mechanical ventilation. Urine samples from the child showed evidence of methadone and barbiturates. The evidence at the time seemed to point towards deliberate intoxication. She was subsequently placed on the child protection register in the category of actual physical injury.

Unsuitable carers
Drug misuse can lead to a variety of non-related adults coming into a drug using home, and some visitors could pose a risk to children. Children might be left with multiple and unsuitable carers, who may not be able to meet children's needs and may pose a risk of abuse.

Child trauma and death
Children of misusing parents might witness traumatic events such as the death of a parent through overdose or murder, or witness a parent being arrested (Kolar et al., 1994). They may be injured in road accidents because their parent is driving under the influence of alcohol or drugs (Black and Mayer, 1980). Child death has also been well documented in children of substance misusing parents (Merrick, 1985; Jaudes et al., 1995; Tyler et al., 1997; Besharov, 1989). In a series of thirteen Part 8 reviews conducted because of a child death, four had substance misuse as a major factor leading

to the child's death (Sheffield Area Child Protection Committee). The following anonymised case illustrates how child death can occur.

Case example
Jake died at one year eight months of severe internal injuries. Jake had been seen on a previous occasion with two black eyes. Two anonymous referrals had been made to the NSPCC alleging that Jake was left alone whilst his mother sought drugs. Both his mother and her cohabitee were heroin users. Jake's mother had decided to reduce her drug habit, and had asked for a referral for help. Her partner admitted hitting Jake and described himself as 'short tempered and ratty' on the day Jake died because he was trying to wean himself off drugs. He subsequently admitted killing Jake, and received a life sentence.

Professional involvement

Shortly after the birth of a baby, there are often many professionals involved with the family (midwifery, neonatology, social services, substance misuse workers) and a profusion of services will be offered. This can be confusing to parents, and therefore needs to be properly co-ordinated. In families progressing satisfactorily, there may be a tendency for services to withdraw involvement once the first few months have passed, which will leave families isolated from professional support at a time when the demands of the child become greater.

Many professions such as police, probation, social services, education, general practice, health visiting, voluntary drug agencies and drug treatment teams are involved with drug using families. Some will be involved with the care of the adult, and some with the care of the child. Professionals need to be aware about the limitations of their roles, for example drug treatment workers may tend to focus on their area of expertise in treating the addicted adult, but will not have the skills to recognise and manage child abuse and neglect. Similarly the paediatrician will need to liase with drug treatment workers regarding the management of the parent's substance use.

Parents need advice and support with the following areas of parenting: general advice on parenting; advice on nutrition for parent and child; advice on safety (especially safe storage of drugs); advice on childhood health checks and immunisations; and advice on testing for blood borne viral infections. Professionals will need to monitor the child's growth, health and development, both intellectual and emotional. They need to ensure routine health checks and immunisations are not missed, and ensure that children are not lost but are followed up.

Assessing risk
Not all alcohol or drug addicted parents physically abuse or seriously neglect their children. There are many components to lifestyle within drug taking families that may predispose to, or protect a child from, abuse. Various factors identified with both higher and lower risks to children are shown below (Tables 2 and 3).

Table 2. Factors associated with higher risk to children

Addicted parent being the mother; (Black and Mayer, 1980, Murphy et al., 1991)
Longer period of drug use (Rothstein and Gould, 1974)
Continuing substance misuse (Berry, 1996, Fraser and Cavanagh, 1991)
Continuing substance misuse in pregnancy (Murphy et al., 1991)
Use of other drugs in addition to methadone (Rothstein and Gould, 1974)
Drug taking affecting lifestyle (Olsen et al., 1996)
Greater degree of poverty (Black and Mayer, 1980, Berry, 1996)
Presence of domestic violence (Black and Mayer, 1980)
Lack of social support (Black and Mayer, 1980, Olsen et al., 1996)
Lower parental education (Jaudes et al., 1995) and parental learning
    difficulties (Berry, 1996)
Very young mothers (aged under 18), and mothers aged over 30 years
    (Rothstein and Gould, 1974)
Infant withdrawal symptoms (Fraser and Cavanagh, 1991, Alison and
    Wyatt, 1999)
Previous child abuse (Murphy et al., 1991, Alison and Wyatt, 1998)
Previous child in care (Rothstein and Gould, 1974)
Poor parenting skills for example in child discipline and knowledge of child
    development (Berry, 1996)

Table 3. Factors associated with improved outcomes for children

Voluntary participation in drug treatment (Rothstein and Gould, 1974)
Living with older family members who are not using drugs (Rothstein and
    Gould, 1974)
Previously demonstrated ability to raise other children (Rothstein and
    Gould, 1974)

The assessment of the combination of substance use, parenting capacity and child welfare is complex and holds many pitfalls (Olsen et al., 1996). It is important to remain objective and non-judgmental. Assessments and planning must be intensive and address not only drug use, but other issues which may be more important, such as poor parenting skills (Berry, 1996). There might need to be a multitude of treatment objectives including health care, drug use, child care, money management, housing. A wide range of services and resources may need to be provided. Some specialist interventions can be very successful if intensive (Jannson et al., 1996, Catalano et al., 1999; Black et al., 1994) and based on a full understanding of the relevant problems including family psychodynamics (Dore and Alexander, 1996). There is a need for development of comprehensive models of care combining input from all disciplines. Where these have been used, real improvements can be made in parenting skills and child development (Jansson et al., 1996; Catalano et al., 1999).

There is also a need to prevent over-optimism from keeping children needlessly long in abusive and neglecting households (Murphy et al., 1991). In the past children of drug addicts may have had multiple foster placements and stay longer in foster care than non-exposed children (Curtis and McCullough, 1993, Kelley, 1992). This will not help children, and adoption should be seen as a real option, as it offers the real chance to reduce the gap, and allow children to reach normal development (Besharov, 1989, Ornoy et al., 1996).

There are fine balances to be made between providing supportive services to substance misusing parents and intruding to protect children. The links between drug abuse and child abuse and neglect are becoming very clear, and we need to be careful to anticipate children's and parents' needs and to minimise the risks to children.

References

Alison, L., and Wyatt, S. (1999) Outcomes of Infants of Drug Addicts, *Abstract from Proceedings of Royal College of Paediatrics and Child Health Annual Meeting*, York.

Baller, K.A. (1994) Office for Children of Drug-addicted Parents, *Acta Paediatrica S*, 404, 75–7.

Bays, J. (1990) Substance Abuse and Child Abuse. Impact of Addiction on the Child, *Pediatric Clinics of North America*, 37, 881–904.

Berry, M. (1996) Services to Prevent Child Placing-out for Cocaine-affected and Non-affected Families, *Child and Family Social Work*, 1, 219–31.

Besharov, D.J. (1989) *The Children of Crack. Will we Protect Them?* Public Welfare. Fall, 6–11.

Binchy, J.M., Molyneux, E.M., and Manning, J. (1994) *Accidental Ingestion of Methadone by Children in Merseyside. BMJ*, 308, 1335–6.

Black, M., Nair, P., Kight, C., Wachtel, R. et al. (1994) Parenting and Early Development Among Children of Drug-using Women: Effects of Home Intervention, *Pediatrics*, 94, 440–8.

Black, R., and Mayer, J. (1980) Parents with Special Problems: Alcoholism and Opiate Addiction, *Child Abuse and Neglect*, 4, 45–54.

Burns, E.C., O'Driscoll, M., and Wason, G. (1996) The Health and Development of Children Whose Mothers are on Methadone Maintenance, *Child Abuse Review*, 5, 113–220.

Catalano, R.F., Gainey, R.R., Fleming, C.B., Haggerty, K.P., and Johnson, N.O. (1999) An Experimental Intervention with Families of Substance Abusers: One-year Follow-up of the Focus on Families Project, *Addiction*, 94, 241–54.

Chan, L.S., Wingert, W.A., Wachsman, L., Schuetz, S., and Rogers, C. (1986) Differences Between Dropouts and Active Participants in a Pediatric Clinic for Substance Abuse Mothers, *American Journal of Drug and Alcohol Abuse*, 12, 89–99.

Chasnoff, I.J. (1988) Drug Use in Pregnancy: Parameters of Risk, *The Pediatric Clinics of North America*, 35, 1403–12.

Chasnoff, I.J., Hatcher, R., and Burns W. (1980) Early Growth Patterns of Methadone-addicted Infants, *American Journal of the Disabled Child*, 134, 1049–51.

Curtis, P.A., and McCullough, C. (1993) The Impact of Alcohol and Other Drugs on the Child Welfare System, *Child Welfare*, 72, 533–42.

Davis, S.K. (1990) Chemical Dependency in Women: A Description of its Effects and Outcome on Adequate Parenting, *Journal of Substance Abuse Treatment*, 7, 225–32.

Dore, M.M., and Alexander, L.B. (1996) Preserving Families at Risk of Child Abuse and Neglect: The Role of the Helping Alliance, *Child Abuse and Neglect*, 20, 349–61.

Famularo, R., Kinscherff, R., and Fenton, T. (19926) Parental Substance Abuse and the Nature of Child Maltreatment, *Child Abuse and Neglect*, 16, 475–83.

Famularo, R., Kinscherff, R., Bunshaft, D., Spivak, G., and Fenton, T. (1989) Parental Compliance to Court Ordered Treatment Interventions in Cases of Child Maltreatment, *Child Abuse and Neglect*, 13, 507–14.

Fraser, A.C., and Cavanagh, S. (1991) Pregnancy and Drug Addiction: Long Term Consequences, *Journal of the Royal Society of Medicine*, 84, 530–2.

Gawin, F.H., and Ellinwood, E.H. (1988) Cocaine and Other Stimulants: Action, Abuse and Treatment, *New England Journal of Medicine*, 318, 1173–82.

Jansson, L.M., Svikis, D,. Lee, J., Paluzzi, P., Rutigliano, P., and Hackerman, F. (1996) Pregnancy and Addiction. A Comprehensive Care Model, *Journal of Substance Abuse Treatment*, 13, 321–9.

Jaudes, P.1., Ekwo, E., and Van Voorhis, J. (1995) Association of Drug Abuse and Child Abuse, *Child Abuse and Neglect*, 19, 1, 1065–75.

Kelley, S.J. (1992) Parenting Stress and Child Maltreatment in Drug-exposed Children, *Child Abuse and Neglect*, 16, 317–28.

Kelley, S.J., Walsh, J.H., and Thompson, K. (1991) Birth Outcomes, Health Problems and Neglect with Prenatal Exposure to Cocaine, *Pediatric Nursing*, 17, 130–6.

Kolar, A.F., Brown, B.S., Haertzen, C.A., and Michaelson, B.S. (1994) Children of Substance Abusers: The Life Experiences of Children of Opiate Addicts in Methadone Maintenance, *American Journal of Drug and Alcohol Abuse*, 20, 159–71.

Larsson, G., Bohlin, A.B., and Tunell, R. (1985) Prospective Study of Children Exposed to Variable Amounts of Alcohol in Utero, *Archives of Disease in Childhood*, 60, 316–21.

Leiffer, M., Shapiro, J.P., and Kassem, L. (1993) The Impact of Maternal History and Behaviour upon Foster Placement and Adjustment in Sexually Abused Girls, *Child Abuse and Neglect*, 17, 715–6.

Merrick, J. (1985) Addicted Mothers and their Children: A Case for Co-ordinated Welfare Services, *Child: Care, Health and Development*, 11, 159–69.

Murphy, M.J., Jellinek, M., Quinn, D., Smith, G., Poitrast, F.G., and Goshko, M. (1991) Substance Abuse and Serious Child Mistreatment: Prevalence, Risk and Outcome in a Court Sample, *Child Abuse and Neglect*, 15, 197–211.

Olofsson, M., Buckley, W., Andersen, G.E., and Friis-Hansen, B. (1983) Investigation of 89 Children Born by Drug-dependent Mothers. II. Follow-up One-Ten Years after Birth, *Acta Paediatric Scandanavia*, 72, 407–10.

Olsen, L.J., Allen, D., and Azzi-Lessing, L. (1996) Assessing Risk in Families Affected by Substance Abuse, *Child Abuse and Neglect*, 20, 833–42.

Ornoy, A., Michailevskaya, V., Lukashov, I., Bar-Hamburger, R., and Harel, S. (1996) The Developmental Outcome of Children Born to Heroin-dependent Mothers, Raised at Home or Adopted, *Child Abuse Neglect*, 20, 385–96.

Regan, D.O., Ehrlich, S.M., and Finnegan, L.P. (1987) Infants of Drug Addicts: At Risk for Child Abuse, Neglect and Placement in Foster Care, *Neurotoxicology and Teratology*, 9, 315–9.

Reno, R.R., and Aiken, L.S. (1993) Life Activities and Life Quality of Heroin Addicts in and out of Methadone Treatment, *International Journal of Addiction*, 28, 211–32.

Rivkin, M., and Gilmore, H.E. (1989) Generalised Seizures in an Infant Due to Environmentally Acquired Cocaine, *Pediatrics*, 84, 1100–1.

Rothstein, P., and Gould, J.B. (1974) Born with a Habit. Infants of Drug Addicted Mothers, *Pediatric Clinics of North America*, 21, 307–21.

Schwartz, R.H., Peary, P., and Mistretta, D. (1986) Intoxication of Young Children with Marijuana: A Form Of Amusement for 'Pot' Smoking Teenage Girls, *AJDC*, 140; 326.

Soepatmi, S.(1994) Developmental Outcomes of Children of Mothers Dependent on Heroin or Heroin/Methadone During Pregnancy, *Acta Paediatrica*, 83, 404, 36–9.

Townsend, P., Phillimore, P., and Beattie, A. (1988) *Health and Deprivation: Inequality and the North*. London: Groom Helm.

Tyler, R., Howard, J., Espinosa, M., and Doakes, S.S. (1997) Placement with Substance-abusing Mothers Versus Placement with Other Relatives: Infant Outcomes, *Child Abuse and Neglect*, 21, 337–49.

Van Baar, A., and de Graff, B.M.T. (1994) Cognitive Development at Pre-school Age of Infants of Drug Dependent Mothers, *Developmental Medicine and Child Neurology*, 36, 1063–75.

Wasserman, D.R., and Leventhal, J.M. (1993) Maltreatment of Children Born to Cocaine-dependent Mothers, *Am. J. Dis. Child*, 147, 1324–8.

Wilson, G.S. (1989) Clinical Studies of Infants and Children Exposed Pre-natally to Heroin, *Annals of NY Academy of Science*, 562, 183–94.

Wolock, I., and Magura, S. (1996) Parental Substance Abuse as a Predictor of Child Maltreatment Re-reports, *Child Abuse and Neglect*, 20, 1183–93.

3 Social Exclusion and Drug Using Parents

Marc Gilman

This chapter challenges current societal assumptions about substance misuse and social exclusion and in particular those assumptions that concern social exclusion and substance misuse among parents or those who have parental responsibility for children.

What is it like to be on the wrong side, on the outside, to be excluded? What is social exclusion and why should *we* (the included) care about *them* (the excluded)? This is the first of a plethora of problems that surround and embrace the social exclusion issue. There are a significant number of us working professionally with families, children and substance misuse who understand working class life and culture. However, far fewer understand the lived worlds of the contemporarily socially excluded.

The source of much of our frustration is our attempt to impose solutions from another social place on problems that are woven into social exclusion. Some sections of the socially excluded in the UK are removed by a distance of three generations from notions of the 'respectable working class'. You can now find socially excluded young people whose grandparents have only a vague connection to the worlds of inclusion and of work. This third generation are born into a world of welfare not of work.

In our post-modern society we no longer employ lady almoners to deal with parents on welfare. Today's version of the lady almoner is likely to be a highly qualified health education professional of a liberal or radical persuasion. These people have colonised several areas of social concern including sex and drugs education. Their ranks swelled following the emergence of HIV and AIDS as a new disease that was potentially fatal and preventable. Moreover, the population didn't know that much about HIV and AIDS, they needed to be educated. Collective efforts directed against HIV and AIDS have been a remarkable success in many parts of the UK. Health educators played a major role in that success.

However, these same educators are having very little success with issues that have been called the 'why not?' issues. These 'why not?' issues include teenage pregnancy and serious drug problems. These issues symbolise the gulf of understanding and communication between the worlds of the excluded and the included.

Why would you become a teenage parent? Why not?

Why would you use heroin and run the very real risk of becoming an addict? Why not? All of the 'why not?' issues are deeply interwoven with social exclusion and the routes that lead to social exclusion. These issues do not lend themselves to being solved by the educational intervention of the most able health promoters. Social exclusion comes about as a result of a whole range of factors compounding each other. Social exclusion represents a package of 'joined up' problems. Heavy-end substance misuse is woven into social exclusion and therefore requires a genuinely 'joined up' solution.

Social exclusion is characterised by unemployment, underemployment, low educational achievement, poor housing, family strains, general break down of community, high crime levels and a high fear of crime. We can picture the routes into social exclusion by ranging many of the factors along a chronological life-line. Theoretically, this line begins at conception and ends with death (but it can carry on into the next generation).

From the stage of conception the risk factors for social exclusion can come into play. But even at this early stage, these risk factors also suggest possible and practical interventions. For example, when a heroin using mother becomes pregnant we have an unborn child of a drug misusing mother. Through shared care arrangements between drugs services and midwifery we hope to institute a care plan that produces a live baby of a good weight, length and head circumference (see Chapter 7). When the health visitors arrive to see the child and mother at home we hope they find a healthy thriving mother and baby.

If this family situation demands that the child be looked after by the social services department, we hope that this is a positive intervention that promotes the child's best interests. Some years later we hope that this child arrives at primary school suitably socialised and ready to be educated. Should problems arise at school we hope that they are dealt with. Should the young person get involved with offending then we hope for a swift and satisfactory youth offending package. Such an illustration (albeit extreme) shows some of the stages that the socially excluded pass through. Unlike the macro global economic forces that produce unemployment, the effects of social exclusion upon families are a series of micro processes that we can influence. Together, in a joined up way, we can improve the situation for children and their parents. We can engineer micro interventions that act as protective factors against the risk factors.

Social exclusion and drug misuse

There are many different kinds of drug use. The kinds of drug use that are interwoven with social exclusion are very specific. These kinds of drug use are characterised by addiction. (Those who object to the term addiction can insert their preferred term.) The crucial point is that recreational drug use exists and has a different social meaning from addiction. Most of us who drink alcohol do so in a recreational manner, our use of alcohol has a different social meaning to the alcoholic's use of the same drug.

Social exclusion fundamentally embraces and frames contemporary drug addiction. The London Drug Policy Forum produced a policy statement that neatly summarises the research and practice evidence in this field. This statement encourages us to be wary of a tendency to overreact to recreational drug use and under-react to problematic drug use. This is critical when it comes to child care assessments. We need to assess a drug user's relationship to their drugs of choice. We do have to be very clear not to overreact to drug use, and some child care systems have been accused of such overreaction. However, in reflecting on fifteen years experience of drugs work, I do feel that many specialist agencies have been guilty of under-reacting to drug misuse. Too many agencies have spun the line that drug misusing parents have difficulties in carrying out their duties as parents because of their chaotic lifestyles. The line goes on to say that drugs treatment for the parents will result in stability and then their parenting abilities can be assessed on a level playing field. This makes good propaganda for drug services, but there are far too many children on child protection registers whose parents are current clients of drugs services (see Chapters 1 and 2). This is especially pronounced where the child protection register includes children neglected, as well as those directly and actively abused.

This is a situation that needs immediate attention. If a high proportion of children are at risk when their drug misusing parents are in treatment, then what is the situation of those children of drug misusing parents not in treatment?

Some drug services have been guilty of under-reacting to drug misuse. They have discharged their duties in isolation in absolute respect of their adult clients, with little thought about child care issues (see Chapter 10). In a political climate that is demanding rigorous enquiry into social exclusion, this practice is insufficient.

In theory, drug addiction can effect anyone without regard to race, class, gender or age. In practice, drug addiction embraces a disproportionate number of the socially excluded. It does this because drug addiction is at heart a 'why not?' issue. William Burroughs told us fifty years ago that 'junk wins by default'. Put simply, addiction fills voids. These voids can be psychological, social, emotional, spiritual and temporal. Mass unemployment is a most efficient way of creating these voids and heroin addiction comes along to fill them. This symbiotic relationship between unemployment and heroin addiction started in the UK in the early 1980s and has been maintained to this day.

Of course there are many individual cases of heroin addiction amongst the rich and famous. These are the exceptions that prove the rule. When they decide to stop using they have plenty of reasons why they should stop and stay stopped. When they clean themselves up they go back to a world of opportunity. When a socially excluded heroin addict cleans up, they return to a sink estate, without work and surrounded by people still 'bang at it'. They soon run out of reasons why not to have another go and another and another. Drug *use* may well be an equal opportunity recruiter. Drug *addiction* is highly discriminatory. We have a very good idea where the majority of tomorrow's drug addicts will come from. They will come from those areas of highest social exclusion. If we want to find many of tomorrow's potential addicts, to best target our prevention efforts, then we must look inside these risk groups.

Risk

The children of drug and alcohol misusing parents are at higher risk, this risk is not just about substance misuse but also about potential family disharmony which may emanate from social exclusion: 'The best predictor of adverse long-term effects on children is the co-existence of problem drinking (or substance misuse) with family disharmony' (Cleaver et al., 1999, p23).

This risk starts from conception. Whilst the baby is in the womb the mother might smoke, drink or take drugs (see Chapter 7). A pregnant woman might be the victim of domestic violence at the hands of a substance misusing father. Many of these high risk children are subjected to some form of abuse before they are even born.

Children with a history of family problems with inconsistent and disruptive parents are at higher risk. Bereavement of a loved one can be a very real cause of disruption. Bereavement of a loved one can be devastating for anyone, but could push an already vulnerable young person over the edge into addiction.

Being looked after, in the care of the local authority's social services department, is often cited as a risk factor for the development of serious drug misusing problems. However, being looked after can also be a risk factor for the other risk factors. Looked after young people are well represented in many of the other risk groups such as non school attendees, school excludees, young offenders, teenage prostitutes, pregnant teenagers, homeless people etc. This suggests a clear need to target the looked after population for early intervention drugs prevention work.

Imagine that a 'normal' teenager (i.e. not a member of any of the other high risk groups) whose parents have died has to be looked after in a children's home. As things stand there is a chance that life in this institution will introduce this child to drugs and crime. (This may be less likely if the child is successfully placed with a foster family or adopted.) One of the most worrying aspects of being looked after is the amount of change and dislocation children experience. Young people who are looked after can be moved from one placement to another at an alarming rate. All children need to feel safe and secure in order to thrive. Being constantly moved from one care arrangement to another undermines this most basic of human needs. One of the most appealing attractions of a drug like heroin is that it is always there and it always does what it says. In a confusing, frightening and ever changing world heroin acts as the ultimate safety net. For the price of a bag, heroin will take you to a safe, warm and familiar place every time. The constant movement of looked after young people increases their chances of encountering all drugs in one place or another. Combine these structural features of the system with the emotional pain that many looked after young people are trying to live with and the relationship between being looked after and drug misuse is all too easy to see.

Assessments

Assessment is absolutely crucial for families with young children and for looked after young people. Action on assessments needs to be guided by the most basic of principles: *try not to make things worse*. For example, being placed in a large children's home, located in a local crime hot spot, staffed by poorly paid and poorly trained agency personnel, all add very real situational risk factors to the most stable young person, it can be a disastrous experience for an emotionally vulnerable young person.

There are cases where being looked after by a foster family or being adopted might act as a protective factor for the child of a drug misusing parent. Staying with drug misusing, criminal parents may be *worse* than being fostered or adopted but *better* than being placed in a children's home.

What can we change?

Having outlined how social exclusion frames substance misuse, I would like to conclude by focusing on things that we should be able to change, both in our own agencies and in existing and future inter-agency partnerships (such as Area Child Protection Committees, Drug Action Teams, Youth Offending Teams and Early Years initiatives). Taken together these recommendations could form a model for early intervention to which we might aspire in the battle to break the links between social exclusion and substance misuse.

The model offered is a Child Concern Model that is very similar to Bolton ACPC's model (Jones and O'Loughlin, forthcoming). It is based around the traffic light concept. The three stages are green, amber and red. At the green stage (Level 1) a health visitor, school nurse or a community policeman may have a low level concern about a child that they wish to share with someone else *within* their own agency. After discussion it might be appropriate to refer the child or family to an appropriate agency or service.

If things do not improve or the concern becomes more complex and requires an inter-agency response, then the amber stage (Level 2) leads to a non-statutory child concern meeting being called and outside agency personnel being invited to contribute to a package of appropriate services for the child and family.

If the concern increases to the likelihood of significant harm to the child, the red stage (Level 3) sees a full blown child protection conference being called, the child's name being included on the register and a child protection plan and core group being established (see Appendix 2). In effect, this model builds in two preventative, service providing stages before formal protective interventions take place.

If the Level 3 stage is reached, 'permanency planning' and 'concurrent planning' systems could be in place once a decision is made that the child needs to be looked after. There are good examples of concurrent planning for permanency. This is particularly pertinent for the children of drug and alcohol misusing parents, who can disrupt otherwise successful foster placements.

In conclusion, substance misuse is not a separate issue to social exclusion but is an integral, intertwined strand that holds a particular potential to seriously affect parents, children and young people at each stage of their career in social exclusion.

We know that drug addiction can be a recurring condition. This is even more pronounced amongst socially excluded families. We must be very careful about uncritically supporting drug and alcohol misusing parents who want their children back from care to have 'another go' at parenting. When the parent relapses the child goes back into care through a revolving door, another emotional scar is inflicted and the young person takes another step towards repeating their parents experience of social exclusion and substance misuse.

If we are to intervene and break this cycle we must put the child's needs and development first. We must support the efforts of substance misusing parents and substance misuse service providers to produce good enough, stabilised, care for their dependant children. But these efforts to improve parenting must be subordinate to the child's separate need for stability and permanency. Concurrent, as opposed to sequential, planning allows for such strategic interventions to be implemented.

References

Cleaver, H., Unell, I., and Aldgate, J. (1999) *Children's Needs: Parenting Capacity*, London: HMSO.

Jones, L., and O'Loughlin, T. (forthcoming) A Child Concern Model to Embrace the Framework in Calder, M., and Hackett, S. (Eds) *The Childcare Assessment Manual*, Lyme Regis: Russell House Publishing.

4 Responsible Carers, Problem Drug Takers or Both?

Eva Elliott and Ali Watson

No child should be left in the hands of a junkie mother. (Sweeney 1997)

Introduction

This quotation appeared in an article in *The Observer* just as our research report on the needs of local drug using parents was being written. The article was about a heroin addict who was pregnant at the same time that the journalist Veronica Guerin was murdered during her investigation of the drug trade in Ireland. The woman in question had since detoxed and was, by all accounts, doing well in a long-term rehabilitation unit but the baby, along with her two older children, had been placed in care by social services. Despite calling for everyone to give this particular mother a break, the writer clearly believed that social services were justified in their actions. His statement urging the removal of children from their drug addict parents was presented without argument, and assumed that readers would share his moral presupposition. But such a view is not widely entertained by those who work with drug users and who recognise that an inability to provide adequate care for one's children can stem from any number of social, economic and/or personal factors which may or may not include a chaotic life-style associated with drug use. Nevertheless, many of the parents we interviewed were concerned that local providers, and most members of the general public, would share the views expressed in Sweeney's article. They believed that the public image of a drug using parent is one which provokes anger, fear and condemnation. In this context it is probably not very surprising that their main concerns focused around the issues of anonymity, confidentiality and unwarranted intrusion into their day-to-day lives.

It is important that services aimed at improving the family life of the children of drug using parents take into account the type of support that the parents themselves would find useful, and it was on such a premise that our research was based. This chapter briefly describes both the project design and the people who took part in the interviews. The views and experiences of drug using parents are then explored in more detail. As many readers are likely to be involved in offering some sort of provision to parents who use drugs, we focus on the reasons they gave for not seeking formal support, and the ways in which they felt that services could be made more sensitive and appropriate both to their own, and to their children's needs.

Design and methods

The research was carried out over a seven-month period during 1997 in a single metropolitan area health authority at the request of the local Drug Action Team, which had identified drug using parents as a priority group for service development. They wanted the researchers to interview current, former and (most importantly to the DAT) non-service users about their experiences and needs as drug users with child care responsibilities. In total 52 interviews were conducted with drug using parents; an almost equal number of females and males were included in the sample. An open interview schedule was used in an attempt to allow the respondents to articulate their own beliefs freely, and to try and identify the links between their personal experiences and the decision-making pathways that they chose, or felt were open to them. Interviews were taped where possible, although most people were understandably reluctant to entrust their recorded experiences to a team of unknown researchers.

Interviews were also carried out with key workers from a range of local generic and specialist services, although these are not described here. Their perceptions of the families' support needs, and the extent to which these coincided with the parents' own views, are discussed in the full research report (Elliott and Watson, 1998).

The interviews with current service users were conducted by the lead researchers, who accessed respondents through a variety of local providers to try and ensure the inclusion of a broad range of views and experiences. However, the majority of the interviews with past users of services, and those who had never used them, were undertaken by four user representatives or 'privileged access interviewers' who were trained and supported by the research team.

The user representatives were local stable or former drug users themselves, and two of the four had some previous experience of conducting research (albeit of a mainly quantitative nature). They used a 'snowballing' technique to access respondents, starting with drug using parents in their own informal networks, then using known contacts to introduce them to other members of the target population.

We feel strongly that the user representatives' involvement was crucial to the overall success of the project. They opened the research to the views of people that more orthodox researchers would, as 'outsiders' to their world, have found it extremely difficult to otherwise reach. Not only did the interviewers know a whole range of drug using parents who were not using services, but they were trusted by people within those networks. The research therefore benefited from an important, privileged and (we hope) honest insight into the day-to-day lives of parents who use drugs.

Although there were also difficulties inherent in involving local users in the research process (in particular around the amount of ongoing support they needed, our sense of distance from the raw data they collected, and our concerns about benefiting from their skills and experiences without exploit-

Table 1. Age of children cared for by respondents

Age of children	Number of children
Under a year	5
1–5 years	36
6–10 years	27
11–15 years	8
16 years and above	2

ing their labour) we would argue that they made an invaluable contribution to the research, and the information they collected was both rich and illuminating.

A description of the user representatives' involvement is provided in the research report, and a discussion of the key issues arising from this and similar methodological approaches is the subject of a forthcoming paper (Elliott and Watson, 2000).

The respondents
The interviewees were at various stages of their parenting careers (see Table 1). While the majority had only one child, almost two-fifths had two or more children they were caring for on a full or part-time basis. Most of these children were still relatively young, although it was interesting to hear how parents' concerns began to change as their children grew older.

Heroin was the drug of use most commonly mentioned, with crack cocaine a high second (see Table 2). The data for alcohol and cannabis are probably

Table 2. Types of drug used by respondents

Drug used (self report)	Number of respondents
Heroin	47
Cocaine	33
Cannabis	29
Amphetamines	22
Methadone	13
LSD	12
Ecstasy	12
Temazepam	6
Valium	5
Alcohol	4
Solvents	4
Magic mushrooms	2

Table 3. Number of drug types used (per respondent)

Number of drug types used	Number of respondents
1	3
2	12
3	13
4 or more	24

misleading, however, as quite a few respondents talked about these only as an afterthought. Clearly some people did not consider cannabis use to be in any way problematic, smoking it in front of the children while being very strict about concealing all evidence of so-called 'hard' drugs from them.

Again heroin was most often cited as the drug of preference, although less than half the respondents actually indicated such a preference. The vast majority described themselves as poly drug users, with 24 people saying that they were using, or had used, four or more different drug types (Table 3).

The interviewees were asked a variety of questions about their experiences of, and views about local services, and the ways in which being a parent affected their contact with these services. It is arguable that many of the issues they raised would apply equally to drug users who did not happen to be parents. What having children appeared to do, however, was to bring some of these concerns into much sharper focus, and it is these that are explored in this chapter.

What the research found
The informal context: being a parent who uses illegal drugs
Before looking at their views on the appropriateness (or inappropriateness) of local services, it is important to outline the context in which respondents lived. The interviews revealed some very interesting and important insights into what life is like for a parent who uses illegal drugs. Most people appeared to have developed quite complex strategies for managing whatever risks they considered inherent in their dual roles as drug users and as parents.

While very few described themselves as full time parents, only a handful talked about receiving formal child care support from nurseries or family centres. Most relied on informal networks and the help they were given by families and friends. It was by no means unusual, for example, for grandparents to look after the children during the week, and for the parents to have them at weekends and in school holidays. This type of support was clearly considered to be very important. As one father said: 'Her mother looks after them for us. God knows what would happen if she wasn't there.'

For some respondents the flexible nature of such informal child care arrangements enabled them to separate their children's upbringing from a lifestyle dominated by drug use and also, sometimes, by crime. It seemed that even in relatively chaotic households, the children themselves were not necessarily subject to unstable and chaotic lifestyles.

Although some people saw parenthood as a barrier to contacting local services, for others being or becoming a parent had motivated them to try and change their patterns of drug use. A number of the women interviewed had stabilised or withdrawn from drugs completely during pregnancy, although relapse soon after the baby was born was not uncommon. It should be remembered, however, that not everyone is able, or indeed willing to refrain from drug use while pregnant (see also Goode, 1994; Hepburn, 1996).

Other respondents were unhappy about the ways in which they felt drugs affected their family life and the role they wished to play as parents. Being a drug user appeared to place relationships with their children at risk in a variety of ways. Some spoke of their guilt over spending money on drugs rather than on the children: 'He likes to go to the roller rink on Friday with [our son] . . . and sometimes you haven't got the money and you feel so guilty that he's spent £20 in the morning [on heroin].'

Others were concerned that their involvement in crime would end in a prison sentence, which would adversely affect family relationships. They also worried that as their children became older and more aware, they would become stigmatised by friends and neighbours for having 'junkie' parents, or would themselves become judgmental of their parents' drug use.

Having children could therefore provide a reason for wanting to control or withdraw from drug use. This was often complicated by the deep association between drugs and coping, however—the drugs themselves were often used as resources for dealing with stressful events or circumstances. Some people talked about heroin 'making me feel safe and feel I could handle everything'. Others said that drugs gave them the energy and/or patience they needed to run a home and look after the children.

So while using drugs might present risks to daily family life, most parents developed strategies to deal with the practical difficulties of managing their dual careers. Many did their best to use at times when the children were out of the house, so school and child care arrangements helped in this respect. When children were around, they tried to use secretly: 'I do it upstairs, you know, out of the way. I don't want them to see what I'm doing. [They] have never seen me put a works in my arm or anything like that.'

For those parents with younger children, issues of safety were stressed, and a number of fears were expressed about how dangerous it was to store methadone and syringes in the family home. As far as the older children were concerned, many of the worries that were voiced centred around how much (or how little) they ought to be told about their parents' drug use, and how this might impact on the children's behaviour and attitudes towards them.

The formal context: the place of services in the lives of drug using parents

It is not surprising, given the three different groups of parents interviewed, that there were mixed experiences of, and perceptions about local service provision. Some of these inevitably related to policies and practices which had been abandoned by the time we carried out our research. The majority of comments, though certainly not all, referred to the two specialist drug teams based within the health authority area.

It is not possible in a single chapter, of course, to cover all the issues that were raised in relation to people's views and experiences of local provision. Instead the focus will be on three of the main themes which emerged and which (based on a review of the literature in this area) perhaps have a wider and more general application: the relationship between lifestyles, parenting and service use; perceived barriers to service use; and the self-reported service needs of drug using parents.

Lifestyles, parenting and service use
Just as being a parent had an effect on users' lifestyles, so both their lifestyles and child care commitments had an impact on their use of (or failure to use) local services. Some people said they found it difficult to combine going out and getting the money for drugs, and then obtaining the drugs themselves, with attendance at set appointment times, and it was the former that was usually afforded greater priority: 'You haven't got the time to go running round to CDTs and then out getting money, it's impossible.'

It was even harder to juggle this with looking after children, and leaving them with someone else could make things much easier. Many respondents showed a marked reluctance to take their children along to drug services, and a number preferred to risk missing an appointment completely rather than 'having to drag the kids along'.

People also noted how they often felt the need to cover their backs with generic service providers, and particularly family GPs, who knew about their drug use. They were worried that their children were more closely monitored for signs of apparent neglect or abuse, and as a result they felt that completely innocent incidents or accidents often required detailed explanation.

But by far the most commonly articulated concern expressed by interviewees was the fear that their children would be taken away from them. This affected both service users' relationships with their key workers (if only in the short term, and whether the workers realised it at the time or not), and prevented non-service users from seeking help in the first place. Despite increasing evidence that drug use alone is no longer considered a reason for putting children on 'at risk' registers or placing them in care (e.g. LGDF, 1997), there remained a strong belief among our respondents that their status as drug users would override any fair consideration of their parenting abilities.

It should be pointed out that, on the whole, those respondents who did have social workers were keen to emphasise the support and understanding they received from them. In most cases social services had become involved with the family before any contact was made with local drug services, and usually (but not always) because of non-drug related problems.

As a result of their fears, some respondents had delayed initial contact with the drug services, and had taken advice from friends or other agencies before talking about their families. As one interviewee said: 'I went to my solicitors [first] and they said go, and don't worry about any questions they ask about the kid.'

Others had only mentioned the fact that they had children *after* they had been set up with a script or other form of support. This may mean that both official databases and the 'best guesses' of local providers underestimate the number of drug using parents on their books.

Barriers to service use

People reported that they were put off approaching or going back to services by what they considered to be overly strict rules and regulations. The regular testing of urine samples came under a lot of fire in this respect, and was mentioned both as a reason for giving up treatment services, and for not seeking formal support at all.

They also worried that staff would be judgmental or would treat them differently as drug using parents. One or two were certainly under the impression that they had been dealt with more strictly than normal because they were users with children; others again were concerned that providers would see them as unfit parents because they used drugs: 'I wouldn't go . . . the people who work there might see us and think, is she capable of looking after that child?'

Fears and concerns about anonymity and confidentiality were very strong, and seemed to be heightened once users became parents. Being in treatment risked public revelation that they were drug users, something they resisted not only because of the impact on their own lives (how they would be viewed by relatives, neighbours, family doctors and so on) but also because of the perceived knock-on effects on their families. Some interviewees were afraid their children would be teased or bullied in school because their mother or father used drugs, or forbidden from playing with neighbouring children as a result. Others were fearful of being rejected by their own children if their drug use was 'discovered'.

Related to this were concerns about what many interviewees saw as unnecessary and unwarranted intrusion into their families' lives by providers from general, as well as specialist services. This applied to questions about the children in particular: 'Instead of me going to a doctors and mentioning my drug use, he would be more interested about my kid and is she eating well and is she going to school and is she going to bed on time, and I don't need it.'

Furthermore, non-service users especially said that they would be unwilling to trust key workers not to pass on information about their children and their drug use to other support agencies without good reason, and/or without permission. The issue of confidentiality had clearly not been sold to many of our respondents.

Barriers to service use which related more to their status as drug users than to their role as parents were also raised. These included:

- The length of time people had to wait between an initial approach to services and their first appointment and assessment.
- Their worries about developing a dual habit if they were given a methadone script.
- Their concerns about inaccessible and/or inappropriate service sites.
- Their impression that some workers lacked the training and personal experience to fully understand their concerns and problems.

A greater involvement of drug users and former users who 'know the score' was called for in the front-line delivery of services. 'The staff . . . are not prepared for the reality of the people they're dealing with . . . they are from a different culture and find it hard to relate to the clients.'

It is worth noting here that in contrast to their contact with social services, peoples' experiences of primary care, and of GPs in particular, seemed to have been fairly problematic. By no means all the interviewees were registered with a family doctor, which in itself raises questions about the level of general health care their children were receiving. There were many who felt that GPs were unhelpful about other types of support they could access, and unsympathetic to their concerns.

Even where doctors were willing to provide scripts, they seemed reluctant to prescribe any other type of medication, and a number of people were angry that they had been left to cope with what they described as 'genuine' health problems unaided because of the label that had been attached to them as drug users.

In light of their worries about service provision, and the barriers to service use they described, we asked all our interviewees how they thought services could and should change to make them more appropriate to the needs of drug using parents.

The needs of drug using parents

For some people concerns about exposing their children to drug services (and as a result to other drug users) were paramount, and no amount of change to on-site provision would persuade them to bring their children to appointments: 'I can't think of anything [they could do to improve the situation]. Even if they had a crèche it's not the sort of place you'd want to be bringing the kids.'

One solution they came up with would be to offer drug using parents more home visits. This would prevent the children from coming into contact with other users, and would also mean that parents didn't miss seeing their key workers when the children were ill or on holiday from school (a fairly common occurrence otherwise).

A number of respondents said they would prefer to meet key workers at alternative, child-friendly sites such as a health centre or the doctor's surgery. These provided play areas and activities, so parents could talk without interruption and without worrying if the children were safe, but were also more 'normal' and anonymous settings for going along as a family group. This ties in with the move that some local services had already made towards providing drug clinics for more stable users at GPs' surgeries.

Some respondents were, in contrast, reasonably happy to take their children to appointments (or were left with no option because of a lack of alternative child care) and would have liked the provision of a crèche or nursery facility, staffed by people used to working with children. Parents forced to keep children with them during appointments with key workers were frequently interrupted, and often found themselves talking in 'coded' language they thought the child would be unable to understand. Special days or half-days set aside by providers just for drug users with children were also suggested.

The need to maintain anonymity arose again here in relation to the location of drug services; respondents called for more discreet and less well-known settings for the local drug teams in particular. Although these buildings did not openly indicate that they were CDT sites, there was a feeling that 'everyone' locally knew what they were, who went there and why.

Interviewees also wanted more easily understandable and more explicit policies on confidentiality, while acknowledging nevertheless that there were certain situations in which other agencies, including social services, should be brought in: 'Somewhere where they guaranteed they wouldn't involve anyone else . . . unless you didn't treat the kids right or something.'

Interestingly, for a very small number of people the overwhelming need for anonymity also overrode any perceived advantages of home visits from drug workers. As this woman said: 'Even if they [key workers] came to you instead someone might call and you'd have to explain who they were, and even without anyone calling the nosy people in this street would get round to asking who it was that was at my house.'

Overall our interviewees would have liked to have experienced greater flexibility and understanding from workers in relation to specific child care issues. For parents looking after school-aged children, the relatively simple expedient of ensuring that all appointments were made during school hours would have made an important difference. It was also suggested that allowances could be made for the fact that parents (and particularly those with very young children) might find it more difficult to be punctual for appointments.

In addition it was considered very important that providers were seen to acknowledge the wider implications that expulsion from services could have for the entire family, and not just for the drug user.

It should be pointed out that some of our respondents felt their drug use was not currently a problem, and was something they could handle on their own. Being able to feel 'in control' was important to them, and a number had devised their own strategies of coping. These included keeping to a tight budget, and keeping away from other drug users whenever possible. The need for formal provision in these cases was therefore not felt to be an issue.

Having said this, some of the non-service users interviewed were clearly finding it difficult to manage without help. By their own admission their drug use was escalating out of control, and they no longer felt able to hold the family unit together in the same way that they had done in the past. Unfortunately in light of their previous experiences of, or prevailing perceptions about services for drug users (often based on information from friends or acquaintances who had had bad experiences themselves), they felt unable to turn to local providers for support.

In conclusion
The parents interviewed for this research suggested a number of ways in which local services could develop to be more relevant and appropriate both to their own needs, and to those of others in a similar situation.

Even where drug users are linked in with formal support systems, unless they are receiving in-patient care such provision is likely to play only a small, albeit significant part in their daily lives. All the parents we interviewed were finding and developing their own strategies of combining child care with drug use on a day-to-day basis, with differing degrees of success. Their use of, or failure to use formal services is bound to depend to a certain extent on how they choose to respond to concerns that they have at particular points in their lives.

What we hope this research has done is begin to shed some light on the everyday experiences of drug using parents giving rise to these concerns. Service providers are unlikely to be able or indeed to want to convince all drug using parents that they need formal help, or that they need to change their lifestyles. However, if the aim is to offer an appropriate service for those parents who do feel they need the extra support, it is important that such services are perceived as helpful, understanding and appropriate.

Some of the suggested changes would inevitably require additional funding which may not be available; others could probably be achieved through the reorganisation and reallocation of existing resources. Our interviews with key workers, (not discussed here), suggested that a number of these issues have already been recognised by local commissioners and providers.

The provision of services is likely to be shaped as largely by national imperatives as by local need. However, it is important that this is not at the expense of a willingness to be sensitive to the concerns and experiences of a vulnerable group of local people who may look for providers' help and support.

Summary of key points
- Almost two-fifths of the respondents were caring for two or more children on a full or part-time basis.
- More than half the children involved were aged between 0 and five years old.
- Heroin was the most commonly used drug, followed closely by crack cocaine.
- The majority of parents were poly drug users.

- Many parents tried to keep their drug use a secret from the children.
- Some raised concerns about the safety of storing methadone in the family home.
- Most relied heavily on the informal child care support provided by family and friends.
- Many parents were reluctant to take their children along to appointments with key workers, but some had no alternative.
- The most common fear was that children would be taken into care simply because their parents were drug users.
- Judgmental attitudes and/or differential treatment from service providers were also a concern.
- Some parents worried that public knowledge about their drug use would affect their children's integration at school and in the community.
- A number of respondents were not registered with a GP, raising questions about their own and their children's general health care.
- More home visits from key workers and/or clinics in child friendly, non-specialist settings were called for.
- Parents wanted policies on confidentiality and information sharing to be explicit and readily understandable.
- Greater flexibility around child care issues (appointments during school hours, half-days set aside for service users with children, etc) would be preferred.
- More involvement of drug users and ex-users in front-line service delivery was also suggested.

References

Elliott, E., and Watson, A. (1998) *Fit to be a Parent: The Needs of Drug Using Parents in Salford and Trafford*, Salford: PHRRC Research Report No 8.

Elliott, E., and Watson, A. (undergoing peer review) Harnessing Expertise: Involving Peer Interviewers In Qualitative Research with Hard-to-reach Populations in *Health Expectations*.

Goode, S. (1994) Heroin Use and Pregnancy in *Druglink* July/August. 13.

Hepburn, M. (1996) Drug Use in Pregnancy: Sex, Drugs and Fact 'N' Fiction in *Druglink* July/August. 12–14.

Local Government Drugs Forum and Standing Conference on Drug Abuse (1997) *Drug Using Parents and their Children: Guidelines for Working with Parents who Misuse Substances*, London: LGDF/SCODA.

Sweeney, J. (1997) The Heroin Heroine, article in the *Observer Review*, Sunday 26 October.

5 The Missing Drug Users: Minority Ethnic Drug Users and their Children

Kamlesh Patel

The woman's children had just been removed from her care and placed in the care of the local authority, the information I read said she was a chaotic heroin user, using and dealing the drug on a daily basis, she was also involved in prostitution and her house had recently been burnt down. None of us had met her yet and as she was not legally represented in the care proceedings, we did not expect her to turn up at court so when this Pakistani woman, dressed in a Salwar Kameez, with her hair tied back, earrings and a nose stud walked past us three times none of us realised that this was the mother of the three children. I'm not sure what I expected her to look like but it wasn't like that. We seem to be having an increasing number of cases involving young Asian children in situations like this.

Guardian ad Litem (1999)

What does a drug user look like; and what does a drug using mother look like? Over the past 12 years I have worked with drug users in a variety of settings, a specialist statutory social work drug team, a residential rehabilitation unit, a street drugs agency and I have managed a range of qualitative action research projects. Through this work I have met drug users from all walks of life and from a range of social groups. It can be difficult to identify particular groups of people as 'drug users', though I am sure we all have our own images of what we perceive to be a 'typical' drug user. It is these images, perceptions and personal experiences combined with the ever-growing research literature that shapes our responses to service design and delivery.

Since the early 1980s Britain has seen an upsurge in the use of illegal drugs. Many reasons have been offered for this increase, particularly with respect to the use of heroin. These include; the shifts in global trafficking patterns in the early 1980s which resulted in the arrival of heroin in cheap and plentiful supply from South Asia; the introduction of the practice of 'chasing the dragon' which obviated the need to inject; the increase in inner-city drug use and the rise in the use of drugs coinciding with a steep economic recession (Pearson and Patel, 1998). ('Chasing the dragon' is the practice of smoking the drug, by heating it on a metal foil and then inhaling the fumes: literally chasing them.) In response to this situation a number of educational and treatment measures were undertaken by the government; one being the pump-priming programme which gave funds to develop a range of community drug services to complement existing hospital and residential provision. Initially funded for three years, many of these services (like their hospital and residential counterparts) mainly attracted and worked with white, male heroin users.

The mid 1980s saw a variety of headlines concerning the changing face of drugs and drug use. Children as young as ten sniffing solvents; people dependant on a range of prescribed tranquillisers; scare stories from the United States about an emerging crack cocaine scene (Kleber, 1988; Stutman, 1989), and a growing but largely ignored problem of amphetamine sulphate misuse (HMSO, 1987).

The 1980s saw the advent of the HIV/AIDS virus, which introduced the concept of harm minimisation and needle exchange schemes across the country (HMSO, 1988), and continued the funding base of many non-statutory drug services. The 1990s brought with it a range of new drugs, including crack cocaine, ecstasy, ketamine, GHB (Gammahydroxybutyrate or sodium oxybate) to name but a few. The white, middle-aged heroin users presenting at services were becoming younger and issues around drug use and pregnancy, community-based detoxification and complementary therapies were being explored. The Community Care Act (1991) placed the responsibility of improving the quality of care provided to those within residential rehabilitation homes to local authorities. General population drug use surveys (Leitner, Shapland and Wiles, 1993), school based surveys (Parker, Measham and Aldridge, 1995) and the British Crime Survey have continued alongside Department of Health Regional Drug Misuse Databases to provide us with vital information with respect to the ever changing drug situation in the UK.

On the whole, drug service providers have responded well to these changes and have developed a range of service responses to meet these new challenges. One of the most recent being the development of early intervention projects, targeting vulnerable young people. It is difficult to identify particular groups of people as 'drug users' or potential 'drug users', though there is now clear recognition that certain people, particularly young people, with a range of predisposing psychological and/or social factors are more at risk to developing harmful drug problems. Young people exposed to these risk factors (outlined below) often have many complex problems. Harmful drug use may affect young people who are likely to be:

- young offenders
- excluded from school or disaffected with school
- in (or have been in) local authority care
- children with a history of family problems and/or abuse
- sexually exploited and abused through prostitution
- children with learning disabilities
- from families with a history of substance abuse
- young homeless people

- young mentally ill people
- young, single pregnant women
(SCODA, 1997).

These groups are not mutually exclusive. Indeed these young people are likely to fall into several groups. A range of economic factors such as neighbourhood deprivation and disintegration and high levels of unemployment underpin these physiological, family and psychological factors.

So why provide this overview? What has this got to do with minority ethnic communities and drug use?

To begin to answer that question we must examine who exactly are 'Minority Ethnic Communities'?

Minority ethnic communities in the UK

According to the 1991 census, just over three million (5.6 per cent) of the 55 million people in Britain are from minority ethnic groups: half the minority ethnic population is South Asian (that is Indian, Pakistani and Bangladeshi). On the face of it, that small slice of the pie chart would not pose many concerns or generate huge interest among policy makers and service providers. However, several important factors need to be noted: the pie chart does not reflect the true demographic nature of Britain's South Asian communities.

Figure 1. The missing minorities

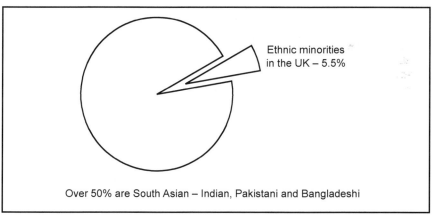

Ethnic minorities in the UK – 5.5%

Over 50% are South Asian – Indian, Pakistani and Bangladeshi

The vast majority of Britain's minority ethnic groups (97 per cent) live in England, mostly in large urban centres, concentrated in some of the most deprived inner-city areas in England. In fact in many of these areas they are the majority not minority population. Secondly, these communities are a young and growing community with nearly half under the age of 25 (this is highest among Pakistani and Bangladeshi communities who have a considerably high percentage of those under the age of 15). In some areas it is estimated that the population will double by the year 2011 within these communities (Bradford Commission Report, 1995).

The very fact that minority ethnic groups are concentrated in urban areas sets in train a number of propensities to suffering from the wider features of economic decline that has affected these regions. The unemployment rates for all Asians in 1991 stood at 30 per cent (as compared to nine per cent for whites) rising to 36 per cent for those of Pakistani or Bangladeshi descent. In some areas those who are economically inactive amongst this group of people is as high as 90 per cent (CRE, 1995).

Much research has commented on the high levels of poverty, deprivation, educational disadvantage, and discrimination in the labour force among these communities (Jones, 1996; Modood et al., 1997). This is coupled with the growing research that points to the over-representation of minority ethnic groups within the Criminal Justice and Mental Health arenas (Clarke et al., 1993; HMSO, 1998). These issues are further compounded by the lack of access to appropriate and accessible health and welfare services.

The latest study from the Policy Studies Institute clearly states that members of ethnic minority groups, particularly Pakistanis and Bangladeshis, are 50 per cent more likely to suffer from ill health than their white counterparts: 'Poor health is associated with poverty. Some ethnic minority groups are among the poorest people in Britain and they have the worst health. They also appear to be receiving poorer quality health care than whites' (Nazroo, 1997).

An examination of the predisposing factors (risk factors) to harmful drug use clearly reveals a worrying similarity to the daily lives of many members of minority ethnic communities in Britain:

It is well documented that there is a disproportionate number of patients from Black and ethnic minority communities currently being treated in high and medium secure services. Over 30 per cent of all patients in medium security psychiatric care, and 16 per cent in high secure psychiatric services are from an ethnic minority group. HSPSCB (1997).

Ethnic minorities accounted for 18 per cent of the (prison) male population and 25 per cent of the female (prison) population. HMSO (1998).

A number of studies have suggested that the numbers of minority ethnic children in care and being excluded from school remains disproportionately high and people from black and minority ethnic communities are disproportionately represented amongst those most vulnerable to homelessness, and the problems faced by young homeless people from those communities are particularly serious.
'Race' and Public Policy Research Unit (1996).

*An increasing number of older people from minority ethnic groups are living alone in poor housing and comparatively worse economic conditions, without support or access to appropriate services.*Butt and Mirza (1997).

> *The incidence of attempted suicides and deliberate self harm among women from certain ethnic minority backgrounds is disproportionately high.* Raleigh (1995).

It is evident that the South Asian community in Britain are prone to a range of physical, emotional, sociological and psychological problems caused by racism, deprivation, poverty and class discrimination. These issues are further compounded by the lack of access to appropriate and accessible health and welfare services. This clearly suggests the presence of all the necessary ingredients for a young Asian person to become involved in the problematic use of drugs.

So why, at the dawn of the 21st century, do we still continue to hear statements that suggest that Asian people do not use drugs?

> *Black people don't use drugs.*
> *The few that do will never inject.*
> *It is a white western disease.*
> *Religion prohibits drug taking: therefore it is not a problem.*
> *If there are any Asian drug users they don't use these services: anyway they look after themselves.*
> *Our strong religious and cultural values stop us from this behaviour.*
> Patel (1993, 2000).

Is it because they have exceptional coping strategies and are able, despite the many problems they face, to resist the temptation of drugs? Or that it is a white western problem that does not touch their communities? Or that the myths of the ever supportive and ever resourceful extended family systems are a reality? Or are these a series of myths that have been a convenient justification for the lack of development of appropriate and accessible drug services for Asian people in this country?

Since the early 1980s, the 'whiteness' of Britain's heroin epidemic was so much taken for granted that social researchers, almost invariably, did not bother to use any system of ethnic monitoring. So drug users from minority ethnic groups (particularly those of South Asian descent) have not and do not feature significantly in any of the general drug population surveys, and continue to be under-represented among known populations of problem drug users.

There are however a number of qualitative research projects (unpublished) examining the nature of drug use amongst Britain's South Asian communities, which have attempted to address the worrying increase in the use of drugs particularly among young South Asian people. These studies (Ahmed, 1997; Awiah et al., 1992; Bentley and Hanton, 1997; Bola and Walpole, 1997; The Bridge Project, 1996; Chantler et al., 1998; D.B.I, 1997; Gilman, 1993; Khan et al., 1999; Mistry, 1996; Patel, 1988; Patel et al., 1995, Patel, 1997a; Patel et al., 1997; Patel, N. et al., 1996; Perera, 1998; Shahnaz, 1993; Sherlock et al., 1997; Patel, 1996) have a series of recurrent themes; these are briefly outlined below.

Some of the service development and delivery issues presented are familiar to those working in the wider fields of health and social care. This in itself highlights the ad hoc, patchy and piecemeal approach that has existed with respect to this area of work for so many years.

Diversity: people are different and have different needs

All brown skinned people living in Britain, who are placed under the umbrella term 'Asian', do not necessarily share the same religion, language, culture or traditions. Figure 2 highlights the complexity of the term Asian.

Figure 2. 'Asian'

Major Religions	Regions of Origin
Islam (4 different sects) Hinduism (range of religious groups) Sikhism (range of religious groups)	Pakistan East Africa India and Bangladesh
Languages and Dialects	
• Hindi • Bengali • Sindhi • Farshi • Boluchi • Gujarati • Bihari • Pushto • Hinku • Marathi • Urdu • Punjabi • Syleti • Kutchi • Telugu	
Different Generations	
1st Generation 2nd Generation 3rd Generation 4th Generation	

What it means to be 'Asian' encompasses a complex mosaic of different language groups, cultures, religious faiths and geographical regions of origin.

In addition, Britain's Asian communities now stretch across four generations, with potentially large gulfs of experience and expectation dividing the first Asian settlers from their grandchildren and great grandchildren. A brief explanation of each generation is offered.

First generation: Asians arrived in this country in the early 1950s in response to Britain's call for additional labour after the Second World War. Many of the young men had no intention of staying and saw themselves as transients rather than settlers, with their strong beliefs in family honour (izzat) and kinship. Their service needs are quite unique and complex.

Second generation: best explained by the following quotation:

> *Shamim is ten. Her parents came from Pakistan to Bradford when she was five. On her way to school each day she walks past fifteen lampposts. She counts them, and at the eighth, she pauses and says to herself; 'now I am English'. On her way home from school, at the same place she says 'now I am Pakistani'.*

Shamim's world is divided into two, with different languages, food and games, and different attitudes to, and expectations of, her as a child, particularly as a girl. She has a foothold in two distinct cultural traditions with different value and belief systems, practices, and histories. But the two worlds are not completely distinct, some things may be the same, and some of the differences may appear to be only superficial.

For third and fourth generations of Asian children the two worlds are becoming even more distinct. The ability to balance one side of the lamp post with it's appealing 'liberal western values' combined with it's unappealing inequality, conflicts with a need to have an identity that reflects their heritage and their familial values.

The majority of individuals are well able to relate effectively to both sides of the 'lamppost' and select the best of 'both worlds', though undoubtedly a range of additional stressors exist for them.

This is not only a matter of generational difference, i.e. age differences; we cannot simply assume all third generation Asian young people share the same experiences and practices, these can differ widely within each generation. For example, in Bradford 52 per cent of all marriages of Asian people were with partners from overseas (Bradford Council, 1998), therefore, those young people from overseas, though they may be the same age, colour and religion may have widely different histories, experiences and practices to the young 'British Asian'. This leaves a complex situation, which needs further analysis before appropriate services can be developed that address the many different types of people and their differing needs.

These demographic and cultural features of the Asian communities point to a range of stressors, which present service providers with a different set of service issues, which they urgently need to acknowledge, understand and address.

Community barriers

Community consultation usually occurs with identified 'community leaders' who have on many occasions posed barriers to drug service development by a strong denial of the use of drugs among their communities. This should not be simply condemned but should be understood as another way of protecting the community from being pathologised and stigmatised as 'deviants' or 'drug pushers'. What also has to be understood is the notion of 'community leaders' and why they may not always be the ideal spokespeople on substance issues.

In the late 1960s and early 1970s many community groups were set up along nationalist lines, i.e. Pakistan Workers Forum, Indian Workers Association, which largely dealt with workers' immigration and housing issues. These organisations grew up around charismatic individuals who were prepared to 'make bridges' between the host and minority communities, thus setting up the notion of community leaders. This had two effects; firstly, when these communities campaigned and became involved in local affairs, the statutory organisations often sought to consult the communities through these 'community leaders; today this practice still exists, particularly in close knit communities. This raises the issue of credibility and accountability as well as effective consultation. Secondly, since organisations were 'all purpose', there was a great deal of resistance to groups which wanted to organise around specific issues (e.g. Asian women's refuges, tackling racist attack units, youth service provision and Asian drug projects). As this was not actively encouraged or supported, many groups did not receive grant aid and the support required to survive in the long term.

Religion

Religion has, particularly for the Muslim community, been raised as an important factor in the fight against drug misuse within the Asian community. Many believed that the reinforcement of the strong religious values inherent in their community would stop the use of mind altering substances. However, young Asian drug users have tended to either ignore these religious values or quite often state that they know that their religion tells them not to drink or take drugs: but no one tells them why (Patel, N. et al., 1997). Drug service providers find it difficult to deal with these religious differences. The potential here is for the problem of Asian drug use to become invisible to both white service providers and the Asian community.

Patterns of drug use among young Asians

In areas where research has focused on particular communities, it is clear that young Asian people do use drugs: and that this use is on the increase as it is in the indigenous population. One worrying trend appears to be the growing number of young people who have developed some form of drug dependency as a direct result of involvement in drug dealing (Sherlock et al., 1997), many tending to use heroin as their first drug of choice.

Heroin and cannabis

Heroin and cannabis have been found to be the most commonly used drugs by young Asians (particularly Pakistani and Bangladeshi males). Though Asian women do not feature in any significant numbers in the majority of these studies, the situation appears to be changing. Several smaller scale studies, which have focused on Asian women, clearly highlight trends to suggest that this is a group which needs urgent attention (The Bridge Project, 1996; Shahnaz, 1993).

The fact that many young Asians do not frequent nightclubs has been offered as a reason by some researchers for the low use of drugs such as ecstasy (GMBA, 1995). However, this appears to be changing, particularly among Indian groups and those who attend organised Bhangra events, where the heavy use of alcohol and stimulant drugs has featured (Patel, Pearson and Khan, 1995). The Bhangra scene was originally a daytime Asian rave or disco which has moved into the evenings and is often organised by university students. The use of a range of solvents and crack cocaine again has been evident among some community groups (Sherlock et al., 1997; Patel et al., 1997; 1999). The drug trafficking routes from South Asian countries of cannabis and particularly heroin is a factor which cannot simply be ignored when examining the nature and extent of drug use in these communities (Patel, 1988; Pearson and Patel, 1998).

Injecting drug users
Various studies have identified the under-representation of Asians at drug services and the low uptake of needle exchange schemes by Asians (Pearson et al., 1993). This, coupled with community beliefs that injecting is an issue for the white community only, and that Asian drug users do not inject, further hampers service development in this area. The question has to be asked: why shouldn't they inject?

An examination of the situation in South Asia quickly dispels the belief that HIV/AIDS and intravenous drug use are only an issue for the western world. There has been a rapid growth in the 1980s of both the use of heroin and the practice of injecting heroin in many Asian countries (particularly India, Nepal and Pakistan). Districts such as Manipur, in North East India, were unaware of Asian intravenous drug users (IDUs) until a major HIV/AIDS epidemic associated with intravenous use hit the area (Wodak et al., 1993). In Pakistan a recent study in Karachi reported a 28 per cent increase in IDU in the city (Parviz, 1996).

Though still under-reported in Britain, injecting is a major issue in places where there are Asian heroin users. The lack of culturally appropriate information and the poor uptake of needle exchange schemes by young Asian people suggest that dangerous injecting practices are occurring (Sherlock et al., 1997; Patel et al., 1995; 1997; 1999).

Issues in service provision
Lack of knowledge and trust of services
The vast majority of people interviewed in these studies were found to have little knowledge of the existence of local drug services and what such services had to offer. Many who experienced problems with drug use would seek help either from their General Practitioner or, in certain circumstances, wider family networks. These findings suggest that the role of primary health care professionals is crucial in determining the take up and use of services by Asian drug users.

Trust, confidentiality and the lack of Asian staff
Overall within Asian communities there is a lack of knowledge about most drugs. The knowledge that does exist is patchy and confused, particularly with respect to risk taking behaviour. Many people in the Asian community are not aware of the existence of drug services and those that are aware, are suspicious and their perceptions about them are usually negative. Trust, confidentiality, and the lack of Asian staff are the biggest barriers to approaching services. These views were primarily based on their experiences

of wider health and welfare agencies where they had experienced discrimination. Even where Asian staff are employed, issues of confidentiality, especially within a close knit community where the 'izzat' (the honour of a family and wider community) could be placed in jeopardy, are a constant concern.

Employment of workers without support
Frequently one black worker is appointed within a team to undertake quite unrealistic tasks. It is unrealistic to expect that one worker can build up trust, credibility, develop and deliver services in such a sensitive area of work within a short period of time, (particularly when organisations have failed to do so over the last two decades). It is also vital that there is senior management support either from within the organisation or externally.

It is important that the worker does not come to be viewed as the 'expert' on every issue in relation to 'ethnicity and race'. It is also crucial that all workers are suitably trained to work confidently and effectively with Asian drug users, thus ensuring that all workers are committed to the development of core integrated services.

A lack of resources is a major long-term problem. 'No black workers', 'no leaflets', 'no extra resources to develop and undertake this work', are all comments that are continually heard; coupled with the lack of enthusiasm from local communities themselves, this means that the provision of drug services for Asian people can easily be overlooked or simply ignored.

Lack of clear direction: getting it 'wrong' despite a commitment
However, there are those agencies that are committed and have secured funds to set up and develop specific projects. A small number have had some success but many have developed further anxieties after their experience in the drug and alcohol field (Patel, 1997a; Alcohol Concern, 1999).

The most common reasons why they have not been as successful as they would have hoped are:

- commitment from senior managers is lacking
- there is no long-term strategic plan
- the issue is placed on the agenda as an 'added extra' or as 'an afterthought' 'an extra burden on an already stretched service': it is not part and parcel of mainstream services

Inadequate, inaccessible, ad hoc and patchy
The difference between white drug users and Asian drug users is that appropriate and accessible services are not readily available: service delivery for Asian users is wholly inadequate, inaccessible, ad hoc, and patchy.

Support for parents
The studies have thrown up a number of recurrent themes with regard to the needs of South Asian families. The lack of knowledge about drug misuse, coupled with community stigma create a high level of fear about drugs. This

often means that drug users who turn to family members for help, or who are 'caught out', do not get the support and treatment they require.

Fears of community stigma and lack of parental knowledge can lead to dangerous practises and solutions (for example 'home detoxification'). In several cases researchers have heard of young drug users being locked in their bedrooms by parents anxious to keep their children away from 'bad company' and hoping that they will 'get better' by being isolated from drugs. The resultant lack of access to suitable medical intervention poses significant health problems for the user.

In other cases, young Asian drug users have been sent to Pakistan or Bangladesh by their family in an attempt to 'remove them from western drug using influences' and 'stop their access to drugs'. Instead the young people have returned some months later with hugely increased drug habits, due to the availability and cheapness of drugs (particularly heroin) 'back home'. Pakistan in particular has a major heroin problem and the use of heroin is now becoming an increasing worry for the country (Ahmed et al., 1993; Pearson and Patel, 1998).

Parents also require access to appropriate information and advice for themselves particularly in respect of their own excessive use of tranquillisers: an issue that has consistently been raised in many of the research studies. This too is an issue that has also been identified recently in Pakistan as a growing area of concern. Early work in Bradford also highlighted concerns around their use of Pann (a green leaf preparation stuffed with either tobacco or betel nut, formed into a wad that is chewed in the corner of the mouth) and Bhang (a cannabis based sweet drink) (Patel et al., 1995). Access to appropriate information is further hampered by the fact that not all Asians read and write their own language, for example in Bradford, less than 28 per cent of the Asian population are able to read and write in their mother tongue. Therefore more innovative methods of imparting information have to be explored, such as the use of audiotapes, debates on Asian radio stations, and videotapes. The Home Office Drugs Prevention Initiative in Northumbria have developed an excellent drugs prevention video tape targeted specifically at Urdu and Bengali speaking parents (NDPT, 1998; Patel, 1999b).

These are simply an overview of the many differences, concerns and issues that need addressing with respect to drug use with the South Asian community. In order to aid the development of a framework from which progress can be made, outlined below is a broad overview of some of the key factors that need to be taken into account to address these issues.

The way forward

Demographic profiling

In the first instance the need to undertake comprehensive demographic profiling is crucial. You must get to know the community that you are targeting in order to begin to understand and acknowledge their different value and belief systems, practices and histories. The Asian community is diverse, therefore a focused strategic approach is necessary; for example targeting an easily accessible user group in a particular area has proved very successful in some projects (Patel, 1999).

Long-term strategic plan with realistic targets

It is important to set realistic targets to establish appropriate services; a 5–10 year strategic plan that clearly identifies short, medium and long-term goals. For example, the employment of a workforce reflecting the make-up of the local population would be a long-term objective, whilst setting up an ethnically sensitive environment would be a short term aim. All too many agencies set very short term time scales and thus place unrealistic pressures on the individual black and minority ethnic workers, which can sometimes result in burnout of the worker and disillusionment within the rest of the workforce.

Multi-agency work

The importance of working in partnership is vital to the process of service delivery to this client group. Multi-agency partnerships will aid in the development of services on a broader setting. They will also enable resources to be shared whilst addressing a range of prevention, education, training, care and treatment issues. Working in partnership with agencies who are already attracting and working with South Asian communities is an ideal way of accessing, consulting and assessing service needs of hard to reach groups.

It is important to note that General Practitioners have been cited on many occasions as the first port of call for most Asian drug users and their families. Drug services need to consider developing appropriate working partnerships with local primary health care teams to ensure effective early intervention and appropriate responses to drug users.

Community development and outreach

A process of community development needs to be undertaken, with a philosophy which is based on equality: equality with the community. It needs to ensure that workers simply do not 'parachute' into communities, fulfil their project aims and disappear leaving only raised expectations. A long-term development, in partnership with the community, acknowledging their concerns and where possible meeting their ongoing needs is essential.

Outreach work is an intrinsic component of community development: activities such as street work, focus groups, education, and information sessions for the whole community have had much success (Patel, 2000). Active outreach within the community raises awareness of services and enables a fuller examination of the drug service needs of the community.

Integrated core service

It is inevitable that the process of service development for many will have to begin by the employment of Asian outreach and development workers and it is important to remember that they will need to be supported and directed in their work. It is also important that an extensive training and dissemination strategy needs to be developed which engenders an ongoing process of joint work and collaboration with *all* staff. Agencies' long-term aim should be to develop mainstream core services for Asian drug and alcohol users.

Information and advice

Previous experience has shown that a range of media and awareness raising activities need to be undertaken consistently and periodically. In addition to developing a range of culturally sensitive leaflets and posters in different languages we need to explore a range of creative and innovative avenues of imparting information to the community. Use of Asian media, especially radio and TV, use of video and audio tapes, drama and music events have all proved to be useful.

Monitoring and evaluation

The whole process needs to be underpinned by a sound method of ongoing monitoring, evaluation and dissemination, otherwise ad hoc pieces of work will continue to be undertaken without lessons being learnt. In conclusion, the majority of the projects that have been outlined cannot offer prevalence estimates of drug use in the Asian community as they were not designed to do so. What they do show, however, is that the pattern of drug consumption among young Asians, particularly with respect to the use of heroin, is an area which needs urgent attention before the problem becomes insurmountable. Substance misuse is affecting a growing number of young Asian people who themselves become parents to another generation of the community. If their needs are not addressed, their well-being and the well-being of their children will be seriously compromised.

References

Advisory Council on the Misuse of Drugs (1988) *Aids and Drug Misuse: Part 1*, London: HMSO.

Ahmed, S. (1997) *Bengali Young Men on Supervision in Tower Hamlets*, London: Inner London Probation Service.

Ahmed, S., Ali, M., and Rafiq, M. (1993) *National Survey on Drug Abuse in Pakistan*. Islamabad, Narcotics Control Division Pakistan Institute of Development Economics (PIDE).

Alcohol Concern (1999) *Developing Black Services: Evaluation of the African, Caribbean and Asian Services Funded under Alcohol Concern's Grants Programme*, London: Alcohol Concern.

Awiah, J., Butt, S., Dorn, N., Patel, K., and Pearson, G. (1992) *Race, Gender and Drug Services*. ISDD Research Monographs 6, London: ISDD.

Bently, C., and Hanton, A. (1997) *A Study to Investigate the Extent to which There is a Drugs Problem Amongst Young Asian People in Nottingham*, Nottingham: ADAPT International Community Centre.

Bola, M., and Walpole, T. (1997) *Drugs Information and Communication Needs Amongst South Asian 11–14 Year-old boys.* A research study commissioned by the Home Office, North West London Drugs Prevention Team.

Bradford Commission Report (1995) London: HMSO.

Bradford Council (1998) *Bradford Local Authority Census Data.*

Butt, J., and Mirza, K. (1997) *Social Care and Black Communities*, London: HMSO.

Chantler, K., Aslam, H., Bashir, C., Darrell, J., Patel, K., and Steele, C. (1998) *An Analysis of Present Drug Service Delivery to Black Communities in Greater Manchester*, Manchester: Black Drug Workers Forum North West.

Clarke, P., Harrison, M., Patel, K., Shah, M., Varley, M., and Williams, T. (1993) *Improving Mental Health Practice*, London: CCETSW.

CRE (1995) *Ethnic Minorities in Britain: Factsheet*, London: Commission for Racial Equality.

Drugs Branch Inspectorate (1987) *Drugs Branch Inspectorate Annual Report*, London: HMSO.

Gilman, M. (1993) *An Overview of the Main Findings and Implications of Seven Action Studies into the Nature of Drug Use in Bradford*, Bradford: Home Office Drugs Prevention Team.

GMBA (1995) *Drug Research Project 1995 Comic Relief*, Home Office Drugs Prevention Initiative and Greater Manchester Bangladesh Association.

HAS (1996) *Children and Young People: Substance Misuse Services: the Substance of Young Needs*, Health Advisory Service London: HMSO.

Home Office (1998) *Statistics on Race and the Criminal Justice System: A Home Office Publication under Section 95 of the Criminal Justice Act 1991*, London: HMSO.

HSPSCB (1997) *A Consultation Event: The Future Provision of Secure Psychiatric Services for Black People*, London: High Security Psychiatric Commissioning Board.

Jones, T. (1996) *Britain's Ethnic Minorities*, London: Policy Studies Institute.

Khan, F., and Ditton, J. (1999) *Ethnic Minority Drug Use in Glasgow. Part Two: Special Problems Experienced and Possible Gaps in Service Provision*, Glasgow: Glasgow Drugs Prevention Team.

Khan, F., Ditton, J., Hammersley, R., Phillips, S., and Short, E. (1999) *Ethnic Minority Drug Use in Glasgow. Part One: Comparative Attitudes and Behaviour of Young White and Asian Males*, Glasgow: Glasgow Drugs Prevention Team.

Kleber, H. (1988) Epidemic Cocaine Abuse: America's Present, Britain's Future, *British Journal of Addiction*, 87, 1351–71.

Leitner, M., Shapland, J., and Wiles, P. (1993) *Drug Usage and Drugs Prevention: The Views and Habits of the General Public*, London: HMSO.

Mistry, E. (1996) *Drug Use and Service Uptake in the Asian Community*, Huddersfield Unit 51.

Modood, T., Berthoud, R., Lakey, J., Nazroo, J., Smith, P., Satnam, V., and Beishon, S. (1997) *Ethnic Minorities in Britain: Diversity and Disadvantage. The Fourth National Survey of Ethnic Minorities*, London: Policy Studies Institute.

Nazroo, J. (1997) *Ethnic Minorities in Britain. The Fourth National Survey of Ethnic Minorities in Britain*, London: Policy Studies Institute.

Northumbria Drugs Prevention Team (1998) *Asian Parents Video*, Northumbria: Home Office Drugs Prevention Initiative.

Parker, H., Measham, F., and Aldridge, J. (1995) *Drug Futures: Changing Patterns of Drug Use Amongst English Youth*, London: Institute for the Study of Drug Dependence Research Monograph 7.

Parviz, S. (1996) *Demographics, Syringe Injecting Behaviour, Abusive Drug Behaviour, Sexual Behaviour and Seroprevalence of HIV among Street Intravenous Heroin Addicts in Karachi*, Karachi, Aga Khan University.

Patel, K. (1988) A Preliminary Enquiry into the Nature, Extent and Responses to Drug Problems (if any) Within the Asian Population of Bradford, *Social Work Education*, 8, 1, 39–41.

Patel, K. (1993) Ethnic Minority Access to Services, in Harrison (Ed.) *Race, Culture and Substance Problems*. University of Hull.

Patel, K. (1996) *It Couldn't Happen to Us* Support Pack; Asian Parents' Drug Awareness Video. Preston. University of Central Lancashire.

Patel, K. (1997a) *An Evaluation of The Clasp Project: Black Alcohol Project*, Preston: University of Central Lancashire.

Patel, K. (1997b) *An Evaluation of the Ashanti Project: Black Mental Health Project, Luton*, Preston: University of Central Lancashire.

Patel, K. (2000) Using Qualitative Research to Examine the Nature of Drug Use Among Minority Ethnic Communities in the UK in Fountain, J. (Ed.) *EMCDDA Monograph*, European Monitoring Centre on Drugs and Drugs Addiction (EMCDDA) Lisbon.

Patel, K., and Sherlock, K. (1997) *Drug Services and Asian Drug Users in England, Scotland and Wales: A Report to the Lancashire Drug Action Team*, Preston: University of Central Lancashire.

Patel, K., Pearson, G., and Khan, F. (1995) *Outreach Work Among Asian Drug Injectors in Bradford. A Report to the Mental Health Foundation*, London: Goldsmiths College, University of London.

Patel, K., Sherlock, K., Chaudry, M., and Buffin, J. (1999) *Drug Use Amongst Asian Communities in Cheetham Hill*, Manchester: Lifeline.

Patel, N., Bamhrah, C., and Singh, G. (1996) *Drug Use in the Asian Community*, Preston: Lancashire Drug Action Team.

Pearson, G., Mirza, H.S., and Phillips, S. (1993) Cocaine in Context: Findings from a South London Inner City Drug Survey. In Bean, P. (Ed.) *Cocaine and Crack: Supply and Use*, London: Macmillan.

Pearson, G., and Patel, K. (1998) Drugs, Deprivation and Ethnicity: Outreach Among Asian Drug Users in a Northern English City. *Special Edition of Journal of Drug Issues* on Contemporary Issues Concerning Illicit Drug Use in the British Isles. Florida State University 28, 1, 199–225.

Perera, J. (1998) *Assessing the Drugs Information Needs of Asian Parents in North Hertfordshire*, Hertfordshire: North Hertfordshire Police.

Raleigh, V. (1995) *Mental Health in Black and Ethnic Minority People: The Fundamental Facts*, London: Mental Health Foundation.

RAPP (1996) *Homelessness Amongst Young Black Minority Ethnic People in England*, 'Race' and Public Policy Research Unit. University of Leeds.

SCODA (1997) *Drug Using Parents: Policy Guidelines for Inter-agency Working*, London, GA Publications.

Shahnaz, I. (1993) *Drugs Education and the Black Community in Lothian*, Edinburgh: Edinburgh and Lothian Drug Action Team.

Sherlock, K., Patel, K., and Chaudry, M. (1997) *Drugs and Ethnic Health Project: Research Report*: West Pennine Drug Action Team, Manchester: Lifeline.

Stutman, R. (1989) Crack Stories from the States, *Druglink* 5:6–7 London: Institute for the Study of Drug Dependence (ISDD).

The Bridge Project (1996) *Drugs and Asian Women in Bradford: A Report of a Survey of Asian Women Aged 14–25*, Bradford: The Bridge Project: A Report to Comic Relief.

Wodak, A., Crofts, N., and Fisher, R. (1993) HIV Infection among Injecting Drug Users in Asia: An Evolving Public Health Crisis, *Aids Care*, 5, 3.

6 Providing Therapeutic Services for Drug Using Parents and their Children

Angie Heal

Introduction

This chapter is concerned with service provision to drug using parents and their children. It uses the example of one service provider, Phoenix House, to illustrate the issues encountered when working with drug using parents. Case studies of real family situations are used to demonstrate how families can benefit from therapeutic intervention.

Parenting skills

There are a substantial number of parents who use drugs who themselves have had appropriate role models as parents or carers, and who have acquired the necessary skills to be adequate parents. Many of these parents will not come to the attention of social services departments at all, as there will not be significant concern about their ability to parent their own children. But there are also parents who, despite understanding their role as a parent, will have a lot of contact with local authority services as they struggle to prioritise the needs of their children against those of their drug dependency. Alongside these particular parents, are a group of parents who have not really managed to attain the necessary attributes of parenting, and who, in addition, also acquire a serious drug problem. These families require considerable input, in terms of time, effort, and resources in the attempt to keep parents and children together safely. As well as needing to address their substance misuse and any psychological problems that often co-exist with drug dependency, we need to be able to offer them more support than to those who are still good enough parents.

Working with drug using parents

At Phoenix House we commonly find that if clients started using drugs before they had their children, they may have rarely, if ever, been drug free prior to coming into contact with our family services. Being newly drug free may present clients, children and workers with a whole host of problems that have not previously been apparent.

Parents using drugs

For clients with children who access our services, we adhere to the standards outlined in the Standing Conference on Drug Abuse (SCODA) document that was developed specifically for drug services who work with families. *Drug Using Parents: Guidelines for Inter-agency Working* is an inter-agency document, and is particularly useful for all professionals involved in child protection and substance misuse. The ground rules for confidentiality (often a very thorny issue in substance work) are clearly laid out and explained for the benefit of all. Sometimes conflict can arise between workers involved in caring for children, and those working with their parents. This is usually due to the fact that drug services have traditionally been very protective of information provided by the client and have been seen to be unwilling to pass that on to other agencies. Services specialising in child protection have sometimes found it difficult to trust that drug services staff will ensure that the needs of children are paramount, especially if it is perceived that a drugs worker would feel that their relationship with the parent might be put in jeopardy.

However, the culture of the drugs profession has changed over the last five years and there is now a different attitude that pervades the work within substance services. Inter-agency and partnership work had already started before the publication of the Conservative Government White Paper *Tackling Drugs Together* (1995), which was followed three years later by the Labour Government's update *Tackling Drugs Together to Build a Better Britain*. Although these are political documents, the partnership philosophy that they contain has been truly embraced by a majority of agencies, working from different perspectives but all contributing to the ultimate goal of reducing the harm done by drug misuse. Phoenix House has taken this new ethos on board, and offers a range of services to drug using parents particularly in the city of Sheffield. These include a residential programme for families and a community-based, family outreach service.

Phoenix House

Phoenix House was born out of the Synanon Organisation in the USA, which was formed in the 1950s. Founded and staffed by ex-alcoholics and drug addicts, Synanon broke the mould of previous treatment facilities which were staffed solely by trained professionals. Using a model known as the concept-based approach, a combination of daily job assignments, encounter or 'attack' groups (where egos, images, and untruths are challenged by other group members) and daily discussions around philo-sophical readings provided a milieu for recovery from problematic substance misuse (Kennard, 1983, Chapter 5). Phoenix House first established a community in New York in 1968 and arrived in Britain a year later. Having started as a single residential unit for adults in South London in 1969, Phoenix House now provides a comprehensive range of services for drug users both in England and Scotland. Although predominantly known as an organisation that offers residential rehabilitation programmes to people who have had a long-term history of problematic substance misuse, a wider variety of services have been developed in the last decade. These include prison rehabilitation units, employment and training packages, outdoor activities programmes, and a range of community services. The residential programmes have evolved considerably since the 1960s, and they have been adapted and changed to suit the present needs of service users and service purchasers.

Previously Phoenix House has worked from an abstinence model, operating from the premise that living life totally drug free is the ultimate goal. For many people that is still the desired outcome and a substantial number of clients attain and maintain such status. But in recent years Phoenix House has come to recognise that becoming drug free is not necessarily realistic for everybody. For some people, limiting the harm done to themselves and others by their drug use and helping them achieve some stability in their lives, may often be far more practical and achievable. It is from such realisation, and also as a result of adapting to a different climate of drug use, that Phoenix House now offers a wider range of services designed to meet the needs of individual clients and their families.

Community-based services for families

The outreach service in Sheffield offers a service to drug using parents who live at home with their children, or who are hoping to be rehabilitated with them, and this service is offered through joint working with social services. The criteria for inclusion is that clients either have to be drug free and need support to remain so, or are still using drugs but are committed to becoming abstinent. Most referrals for this service come from social services, but others may come from GPs, health visitors, midwives, the community health substance misuse team and probation officers. A number of clients also self-refer. As a majority of the client/family contact takes place in their own accommodation, a detailed assessment is made of the home circumstances before a member of the team arranges to visit.

The family outreach service also works with families who are being re-settled in Sheffield from the other Phoenix residential projects. Some of these will previously have been residents of Sheffield who have decided to remain close to families, others will have come from other parts of the country and decided that their best chance of success lies in staying in Sheffield with their children. Some families will have been referred to the service as they have already been identified as appropriate for admission to the Phoenix Family Centre, and so work will be carried out with the parents and children preparing them for admission. A number of issues are addressed before hand such as stabilising or reducing drug use. Four weeks notice has to be given on any existing accommodation, and arrangements are made for the flat or house to be cleared so as not to incur any (further) arrears. If children are either being accommodated elsewhere or being admitted to the family centre, it often means ensuring that there is a smooth transition of school placements, causing minimal disruption to children who have often seen a lot of change already. All these issues must be co-ordinated so that there is a relatively easy admission to the residential unit for both parents, who are newly drug free or about to start a detoxification, and their children.

However, the majority of families that the outreach service work with are not likely to come into contact with the Phoenix House residential unit. These families remain at home in Sheffield with varying degrees of support from all the agencies involved. For some families, family outreach may be the only service that they require, as there may not be any child protection concerns. Parents can, and do, use drugs without risk to their children. Once a family has been referred to the service, then a visit is arranged as soon as possible to carry out a detailed assessment. Information is sought from the parents about their substance misuse, and a criminal, social, physical, familial, and psychological history is also taken. Included in the assessment is information about children, their educational, behavioural, physical and emotional needs and any other professionals involved in their care. As a part of the assessment the confidentiality contract is explained to parents, telling them that information they give is confidential and will only be broken if there are any child protection concerns, or if staff feel clients are a risk to themselves or to other people. In practice most clients are usually quite willing to share what is currently happening within the multi-disciplinary forum. It is also explained that an automatic check is carried out with the Child Protection Unit at Sheffield social services to verify any social services involvement. Social workers will also check with our service to see if their clients are known to us. This is a part of improving communication between agencies where child protection and substance misuse are an issue. As well as working to the SCODA guidelines, the service has drawn up a protocol with Sheffield social services department, which provides detailed information for staff to act upon if they have any child protection concerns.

Once an assessment has been carried out, a care plan is drawn up with the parents that addresses a number of issues. Firstly, drug use is identified as the main area of our involvement either as relapse prevention work, or by stabilisation or reduction/detoxification. Secondly, an exploration of the effects of parental drug use on the children is an essential part of the service. Using the SCODA assessment procedure, information is given to parents about the possible effects of drug use on their children and parents are given a chance to discuss such issues with professionals who understand about drug use and the risks involved. It is often apparent that parents do not know what it is that social services are looking for in terms of risk to their children. Through a detailed discussion with the drugs worker it is hoped that there will be increased understanding and preventative action can be taken in the future. Offending behaviour is also examined, what types of offences, if any are being committed and what effects this could be having on the children. Although there is a definite correlation between reducing/ stopping drug use and a reduction/cessation in drug related offending, other offences may still be committed which need to be addressed in the care plan. Other areas that are commonly identified in plans include unstable/ unsuitable accommodation, DSS problems, and issues concerning debts and rent arrears. These often involve a referral to other specialist agencies. Another part of the care plan will entail establishing areas of leisure or career interest for parents, supporting them in their efforts to pursue new directions in order to increase their feelings of self-esteem and confidence. Attending part-time college courses and leisure centres are encouraged, as well as identifying cheap, accessible days out for families in the local area.

The outreach staff will be a part of any core group that takes place as a result of child protection intervention by social services. We also attend case conferences and reviews, and provide reports about our work with the family for family or criminal justice courts. Through this work we are part of the ongoing inter-agency process of assessing risk within a family.

Although the emphasis of the Family Outreach Service is providing support to parents, it is essential that staff involve the children and extended family as well. As most visits take place within the family home, the worker usually gets to meet everyone that is of significance for the parents. The fact that the worker comes to their home is popular for a number of reasons (see Chapter 4). Firstly, clients do not have to leave the house to visit an office base, it does not cost money and they do not have to brave inclement weather. Consequently, clients are more likely to keep appointments. Secondly, they can avoid other drug users (this is particularly useful if they feel intimidated, owe people money, or want to avoid the temptation of being offered drugs when trying to detoxify or remain abstinent). Thirdly, it alters the power relationship between worker and client as the worker is a guest in their territory. This enables the client to feel more in control and on a more equal footing with the practitioner.

Because of the trust that usually builds between client and worker, children often come to accept staff as people who are supporting their parents in trying to improve life at home. There is often a tangible difference in a parent's relationship with their drugs worker compared to their relationship with other professionals. Children perceive that barriers are less evident and react accordingly, giving the outreach worker a greater insight into the realities of the home situation. Staff are therefore better placed to help parents come to realise what is acceptable behaviour in terms of their drug use and lifestyle when there are children to consider. It need not necessarily involve significant resources to improve a child's routine and care. Ensuring that parents have alarm clocks, to improve late attendance at school may help, as well as encouraging early bedtimes. Parents may appreciate the involvement of 'befrienders' or volunteers, who may have been drug users themselves in the past, who can support the client in attending medical or legal appointments. Applications can be made to charities for grants for children in need. Referrals can also be made to young carers projects, who work specifically with children who have become the main carers in families where the parents are unable to take that role.

Inappropriate responsibility and activity of children

When children live in a family whose lifestyle is heavily influenced by substance misuse, they may become caught up in that lifestyle in inappropriate ways. Children often end up in the role of caring for their younger siblings, their parents, or themselves. These children may engage in cooking, bathing, putting younger children to bed, and ensuring they are up and taken to school. They may fetch and carry for their parents when they are either under the influence of drugs or withdrawing. Children may also feel they have to cover up for their parents, either to social workers, extended family members or the police. They have to work out when they have to lie and when to tell the truth and to whom. They may find them 'gouched out', semi-conscious, overdosed, or dead. They may witness adults using drugs, usually by smoking or injecting, or they may be regularly banished from rooms whilst such activities take place. Even if they can't see what is going on, children are often intrigued or concerned by what their parents are doing. They may never be able to predict whom, if anyone, is at home when they arrive from school, and in what state they will be. Children may be in danger if drugs or other medication are not kept securely out of their reach and may take drugs in a form of imitation of their parents. If a parent sells drugs, strangers may be in the home, the police may occasionally raid and sometimes a parent can be arrested and the children won't know when they will be returning home. Some parents may take their children with them when they are earning money for drugs (shoplifting, stealing purses or selling stolen goods for example) or else children may be actively encouraged in petty crime. As a result children may be taken into custody with their parent and have to spend time at the police station until they are released. Some mothers may be involved in prostitution, either through working the streets, in saunas or in the home. This may lead to children either being left alone, cared for at night by others, or having to leave the house if clients are brought home. They may be placed in vulnerable situations if strangers are being brought to the house for sex. All this can make it difficult for a child to take their friends home, as they do not want to be embarrassed by their parents' behaviour. This can result in social isolation and children becoming loners, or spending time solely with other drug users' children. Life can get very complicated and unpredictable for children in such circumstances, and this may result in truanting from school, difficulties in forming friendships, or other social difficulties. Having allocated workers dedicated to supporting the child through their difficulties can often ease the situation for them, especially if it is in conjunction with increased support at home from other agencies. The scenarios pictured above are often worse case situations and it would be very unfortunate to find them all existing within one household. However, professionals should be aware of what may happen when parents misuse drugs and be able to act to limit any form of adversity that a child may suffer as a consequence.

Case study 1
Tina worked with family outreach for nearly two years. She was 23 years old when first referred and had two children, James aged seven and Janie who was five. Her partner of nine years, Gary, aged 22, was serving a four-year custodial sentence for armed robbery. They had been using heroin for the past five years. The situation had deteriorated at home following Gary's imprisonment, Tina was finding it difficult to cope with looking after two young children whilst funding and maintaining a £40 daily intravenous heroin addiction. Her probation officer became concerned at her ability to adequately care for her children, and contacted social services. At the initial case conference the children were placed in the Neglect category of the Child Protection Register. Tina was then referred to the Family Outreach Service. During the first nine months of contact, Tina had three short spells in prison for shoplifting and theft offences, all to fund her drug habit. The children were placed on interim care orders, and went to live with their aunt whilst Tina tried to prove that she could remain drug free. Unfortunately this was not the case, and the situation deteriorated rapidly once Gary was released from prison. The effects on both children were evident; their behaviour and health improved considerably once they had been placed with their aunt. Full care orders were obtained and long-term foster placements were sought and found. Both parents are now doing very well in a residential rehabilitation unit. They have regular contact with the children and if all goes well in the next year there will be another attempt at rehabilitation for the family. Whilst working with the family, the family outreach worker visited weekly, or more in times of crisis. She was an integral part of the core group, made referrals to other agencies including GPs, community drug teams, residential units, completed full needs assessments and wrote court reports and advocacy letters. She built up a relationship with Tina and Gary that enabled her to gain a degree of insight into their lives that few other professionals would have been allowed. This gave her the opportunity to help them understand the effects of their behaviour on their children, and ultimately their survival as a family.

The family centre

This service provides a package of residential care where parents who have a serious drug problem can be accommodated with their children, during a six-month rehabilitation programme. The aims and objectives of the service include:

- Supporting adults with a structured programme in order to be able to cease their dependence on drugs and alcohol.
- Providing a safe and stimulating environment for all members of the family, especially the children.
- Assisting parents to learn parenting skills; and providing an environment in which the family can live together, with support from trained staff. This gives them a realistic chance of dealing with their problems and an opportunity to remain together safely in the future.

A detoxification programme is available on admission through the medical practitioners. At the family centre parents are responsible for the care of their children at all times throughout their stay. It is clear to all that children are not entering the 'looked after' system. However, during the detoxification period, there is increased staff support to enable parents to care adequately for their children whilst experiencing withdrawals, but also to help them settle into the programme. Staff also monitor standards of care, the safety of children, and the progress being made by parents.

As part of the admission procedure, a care plan is drawn up with the funding authority and detailed objectives and goals of the placement are established for the family as a whole as well as for individual members. These outline responsibilities, tasks to be undertaken, goals to be achieved and the framework for review. Each family member has their own allocated keyworker and one member of staff takes overall responsibility for co-ordinating and monitoring the progress of the family. Where the goals of a care plan are not being met, or where other needs emerge, there is immediate liaison with the funding authority. If it appears that a substantial departure from the care plan is necessary then a review is called, where all relevant persons are expected to attend. Each family has their own designated living space, but they share kitchens, lounges, and laundry facilities. Parents are assisted to plan meals, budget and prepare nourishing, good food. They are expected to establish routines of family life with staff giving practical and emotional support where necessary.

Working with children

Despite the fact that parents are at the family centre because of a drug problem, the emphasis is always on the needs of their children. Therefore parents are supported in learning to put the needs of their children over and above their own perceived priorities. Children at the family centre are helped to overcome some of their own personal difficulties through a number of different structured interventions with staff members. Staff are employed to undertake nursary work and direct play with children. This enables them to express themselves on an emotional level as well as develop social relationships with other children. Parents are encouraged to participate in playroom sessions to learn about playing with and nurturing their children. Children are also supported through groupwork and individual key work sessions, and for those who are of school age there is good liaison between parents, staff and teachers. Any identified special needs that a child may have will be addressed through their personal care plan.

Dealing with substance misuse

Parents are given assistance in a number of ways to deal with their substance misuse. They are helped to understand how their drug use has affected their ability to provide a stable environment for their children. They examine how the responsibilities of caring for children may be incompatible with drug dependency and its associated lifestyle. Parents are given individual and group support to learn about the nature of drugs, the harm they can do, an understanding of why individuals use drugs and how to cope with life whilst abstinent. Many people make the assumption that people who use drugs are very knowledgeable about all aspects of their use. This is frequently not the case; it is essential that this opportunity be taken to educate clients about the substance issues. Parents are also helped to develop strategies to remain drug free or to deal with the consequences of relapse. This ties in with the drug education programme, so that people can make informed choices about their lives once they understand the relevant facts. Staff will work with relapse, but if this is frequent or there are child protection issues as a result, then a review will be called. If it is necessary to terminate a placement at the family centre because of continuing drug use, every effort is made to plan for this and for alternative services to be made available.

Sometimes fundamental child care issues have been overlooked by parents, not usually due to wilful neglect but more as a part of a disorganised, struggling to cope lifestyle. Most parents will admit that they find it difficult to cope with their children when they are withdrawing: using drugs and finding the money to buy the drugs often takes priority, as they believe that this is the only way that they can adequately care for their children. By working through these issues, parents may recognise that they have actually been putting their drug use before the needs of their children.

Risk assessment and court proceedings

The local authority and the parents are responsible for the management of risk during placements at the family centre. Our workers contribute to the risk assessment process, this includes specialist input from substance misuse and child development workers.

Sometimes families will be going through the court process during their placement at the family centre. This may be as a result of criminal prosecution, or of court proceedings taken by the local authority concerning the care of the children. We contribute to these proceedings, through submitting court reports and appearing as witnesses. We also support parents going through this traumatic and stressful process, especially if they are newly drug free.

Counselling adults

During key work sessions we assist adults to identify problematic areas of their lives and support them in developing positive strategies for better coping with them. Many residents have had profoundly damaging experiences that require referral to outside agencies to get more specialist input. If the family is settling in Sheffield, then counselling can carry on uninterrupted. If they move to another area then liaison will take place with agencies in that area, so that the client can make links with counsellors with whom they can build new relationships.

Positive approaches to health care

Improving health is an important outcome for both parents and children. The greatest single contribution to improved physical and psychological health for adults is to stop misusing substances. But as parents may have previously overlooked their own physical health and the health of their children, an initial medical examination and follow-up checks for all the family are an important part of the rehabilitation process.

The outdoor activities programme

An integral part of both services is the outdoor activities programme. We employ a dedicated outdoor activities organiser whose role is to plan activities that offer a stimulating and challenging experience, this is seen as an alternative to the 'buzz' of substance misuse. The programme includes climbing, abseiling, caving and walking involving an approach that encompasses team building, learning new skills, developing self-esteem, confidence and leadership. The programme concentrates on developing the abilities needed to participate in such activities rather than promoting a feeling of instant gratification that replicates drug use. A conservation programme is also in operation in conjunction with environmental projects in a variety of locations in Sheffield. Again, this project involves learning similar skills but also helps develop respect for the environment and an appreciation of the outdoors. An evening climbing club is now in operation at one of the indoor climbing walls in Sheffield. Clients use this facility who enjoy climbing and want to develop their skills, but it has also proved an invaluable source for peer support. Having the opportunity to share experiences of caring for children drug free is essential and this has now developed into the formation of another group for abstinent parents and their children. Activities are also offered during the school holidays that are child focused. Making the most of the nearby Derbyshire countryside, the Outdoor Activities Organiser plans trips in conjunction with the parents and the residential staff. Sessions are also held with environmental groups that encourage children to learn about the countryside and nature. Other activities such as swimming, playing sports and walking, are planned by each family for the benefit of the children.

Re-settlement and aftercare

If families are re-settling in Sheffield, the residential keyworker, the family outreach worker, and any social workers that are involved, put together a care plan with parents that supports them being re-housed with their children. This includes helping parents find suitable accommodation, schools, nurseries, GPs and any other services that may be of assistance.

Parents who complete the residential programme are encouraged to return to their home town for re-settlement. Although there are risks involved in terms of being back in old drug using areas, and seeing old acquaintances, vital extended family support will usually be available. This is very important in terms of support for both parents and children at a time when there is a lot of stress within the family. Also if the family situation deteriorates considerably, children may be placed within the extended family rather than with foster parents of children's homes in an unfamiliar city. Many children understand the issues involved and their wishes need to be taken into consideration. The situation becomes that much harder if children act out against a decision that they feel they have not been involved in making.

In a situation where parents previously used drugs to escape from stresses a lot of work is needed around relapse prevention to ensure that old negative coping strategies do not suddenly seem attractive again. Usually the new family situation settles down after the initial period of flux, and with professional support and intervention the family will hopefully get into a routine that is positive and workable. If the situation deteriorates, social services may need to intervene to ensure the safety of the children.

Case study 2
Tanya had had a serious drug problem for the past fifteen years, and had a related chaotic lifestyle. She funded her habit through a mixture of theft, fraud, deception and prostitution. She was an intravenous heroin user, scripted from the local drug clinic but regularly using other drugs as well. Benjamin was three years old when the family outreach worker became involved. He was a cause for concern for the paediatric consultant due to delayed developmental growth and behavioural problems, and was registered under the Neglect category of the Child Protection Register. Tanya was adamant that she did not want to go to a residential unit, so the outreach worker did not discuss this as an option until she started asking questions six months later. After one year Tanya and Benjamin were admitted to the family centre. Tanya completed the programme having made excellent progress, even though she had never been drug free in the previous fifteen years. Two and a half years later, Tanya is still drug free. She met Adam, a single father in the family centre and, on completing the programme, they moved into a house together with their children. Benjamin was de-registered one and a half years ago. Tanya gave birth to a healthy baby girl last year. She works for a local voluntary agency as a receptionist; he works for a local building firm. They share child care arrangements.

Case study 3
Richard and Sheila were admitted to the family centre with their two-year-old son, having arrived from a city in the South of England. They had a seven-year history of heroin addiction, and Kyle was on a full care order due to concerns of neglect and physical abuse from Richard. They only remained at the centre for two weeks. Richard managed to locate a block of flats a mile away where drugs were easily available, and he made a couple of trips there during his stay in Sheffield. Staff confronted them about their drug use, which they denied and then stated they were returning to their hometown. Their social worker was contacted and informed that the placement hadn't worked out and that they would be returning the following day. Although they acknowledged the concerns about Kyle, Richard and Sheila felt unable

to address their drug problem at that time. They returned home to discussions with their social services department about what the future held. In Sheffield there are many parents who are now drug free or stable in their drug use as a result of them being able to positively use inter-agency intervention and assistance. However, it is impossible to predict who will be successful in achieving their aims and who will not do as well. Some of the most chaotic, drug using parents achieve change and are now in regular employment, with their children doing well at school. Therefore it is essential that everyone has the opportunity to access relevant services when they need them, and are given ample encouragement to make the necessary changes for themselves and their children.

The impact on staff

Working with drug using parents and their children is often extremely stimulating, rewarding and enjoyable work. People who have used drugs for a number of years have often adopted a very innovative approach to life, and have developed a correspondingly healthy sense of humour to help them cope. Both parents and children often appreciate the interventions of staff, understanding that workers have their best interests at heart whilst still retaining a professional distance. Workers understand the issues of their drug use without being a part of the drug scene itself. However, working with drug users, as with any other group of vulnerable people, can be very stressful and emotionally demanding for workers. Clients may need to share significant details of trauma, both past and present. They may also cause distress to other people as a result of their actions. Staff may also be concerned about the welfare of the children and whether they have taken the appropriate action to ensure their safety. Such highly charged issues become a part of daily life for drug workers. Therefore it is essential that staff receive regular, good quality supervision to minimise the effects of working in such a stressful environment. An adequate induction period is essential when starting a new post, to ensure early confidence in service delivery. Regular supervision that deals with professional and emotional issues is vital for the emotional well-being of staff, combined with regular appraisals for assessing work-related performance. A commitment from the organisation to their employees in terms of training is also a necessity. This ensures staff adopt good standards of practice, keep informed of new developments, and gain qualifications that can improve their career prospects in the long term.

References

Kennard, D. (1983) *An Introduction to Therapeutic Communities*, International Library of Group Psychotherapy and Group Process.

Standing Conference on Drug Abuse (1997) *Drug Using Parents: Guidelines for Inter-agency Working*.

7 Substance Misuse and Pregnancy

Faye Macrory and Fiona Harbin

Introduction

This chapter will consider the predominance of drug use during pregnancy, the trends in this area, and how pregnancy and drug use are viewed by society. Consideration will be given to the guidance and policies available to professionals covering service provision for pregnant women who are drug users and how this has been interpreted in practice. There will be further exploration of examples of good practice in Britain and how this has impacted on the service provided to this specific group of women.

Many women use drugs during their pregnancies. These may be prescribed drugs, over the counter drugs, illegal drugs, cigarettes or alcohol. This chapter will concentrate on those women who are dependent users of illegal drugs, predominantly heroin, amphetamine, cocaine and crack cocaine.

For many, illicit drug use is a chronic relapsing condition, and clients presenting for treatment will invariably have been using drugs on a dependent basis for several years. Some women use differing combinations of prescribed and non-prescribed medication. The treatment of drug misuse must therefore be a planned exercise, and not treated as a medical emergency, although it may present on occasions as an emotional and psychological one (Macrory, 1997).

Prevalence

It is very difficult to give a clear picture of the number of women drug users who are pregnant. For many reasons their drug use may be concealed and they may not choose to come forward for treatment (Mountenay, 1999, p7). However it is known that approximately 30 per cent of registered addicts are women of child bearing age (Mountenay, 1999, p7). There is now a decreasing gap between the numbers of men and women registered for drug treatment and, amongst the fifteen to nineteen-year-old age group, there are nearly as many women as men using drugs (Drug Misuse in the North West of England, 1997). For the first time since figures were collected: 'young women are almost as likely as young men to experiment with illegal drug taking' (Bates et al., 1999, p4). A 1996 household survey found that 4.2 per cent of women reported current use of an illicit drug.

This use inevitably impacts on pregnancy. Studies from the United States suggest that one in ten infants may have been exposed to illicit drugs in utero

(Howard, 1997). Ten years ago, a report by the Advisory Council on the Misuse of Drugs (1989) recognised a likely increase in the number of pregnant drug users (Siney and Morrison, 1995) and Mountenay (1999) reports that hospitals have generally indicated an increase in the number of babies born to mothers using a variety of drugs (particularly opiates).

Impact of maternal drug use on the foetus and newborn
There are many difficulties in providing clear information about the impact on the foetus and the newborn of maternal drug dependency during pregnancy. Concentrating specifically on maternal heroin use, Leopold and Steffan (1997) give a list of possible implications for the newborn. The list details the symptoms of Neonatal Abstinence Syndrome:

- general irritability
- hyperactivity
- abnormal sensitivity to touch
- accelerated cardiac action
- an increase in the respiratory rate
- changes in the sleeping/waking rhythm
- wild sucking at their fists
- shrill and excessively long phases of screaming tremors

- shivering
- sneezing
- perspiration
- fever
- vomiting
- diarrhoea
- inhibited feeding
- in extreme cases general convulsions

This exhaustive list is similar to the indicators identified on the score charts used to assess opiate withdrawal symptoms in newborn babies in many health Authorities.

Without detailing the impact of specific drugs, there is an agreed view that illicit and prescribed drugs can alter pregnancy outcomes and that drug using women have potentially high-risk pregnancies (Hepburn, 1999). As well as neonatal abstinence syndrome there is a risk of higher perinatal mortality and morbidity, due largely to low birth weight and pre-term delivery. There is also a greater risk of cot deaths (Hepburn, 1999) and higher than normal risk of congenital abnormalities (Priest and Attawell, 1996, p162). However, Hepburn (1996) suggests that there is a lack of comparative literature considering the outcomes for the babies of socially included women who use drugs during their pregnancy, and that contributory social factors during pregnancy may have as great a part to play in pregnancy outcomes as drug use.

There is some agreement that neonatal withdrawal symptoms are largely dose dependent (Hepburn, 1999), with approximately 60 to 80 per cent of babies born to heroin dependent mothers showing signs of withdrawal (Leopold and Steffan, 1997). This should not, however, be used as a reliable indicator. Physical withdrawal in a new born baby is usually noticeable after 24 hours and before 72 hours and may be treated with small amounts of morphine (Howard, 1997). Medical and professional advice to women using drugs during pregnancy is generally to stabilise their drug use (where possible, with prescribed methadone) or to stop the drug use with obstetric support, if that is what they prefer (Hepburn, 1996, p13).

One of the difficulties in measuring the impact of drug use on the foetus and the newborn is the other external factors which play their part in the course of the pregnancy. Researchers in the United States have faced a fundamental problem in interpreting the data available and separating the effect of prenatal drug use from the effects of an array of other social and biological burdens that often accompany drug dependence. There is a strong likelihood that the drug user has come from a background of socio-economic deprivation, with poor diet, low income, poor housing, poor access to education, and exposure to violence. This, coupled with use of tobacco and alcohol, can have a major impact on growth retardation for this group of children (Howard, 1997).

Longitudinal studies of affected children are uncommon, as separating the social situation from the effects of the drug used during pregnancy is difficult. Experience in the United States has found that the children who were exposed to cocaine in utero were more likely than others to have medical, educational and social difficulties. However it is difficult to conclude that this was solely due to cocaine exposure, without also recognising social and environmental factors. Leopold and Steffan (1997) indicate: 'the worse the living conditions and the more hazardous the lifestyle the more negative are the effects of the drug on both the mother and child' (p6).

As well as these environmental and social factors some researchers have found it more difficult to publish work on drug use and pregnancy if the outcome of this research is not in agreement with the more negative stereotypes held by society. Priest and Attawell (1996) state that: 'research reporting adverse effects was more likely to be published than that reporting an absence of such effects' (p167).

The impact of pregnancy

Pregnancy has an impact on all our lives to a greater or lesser degree. Great emphasis is placed on the pregnant woman and the important role she plays in the perpetuation of our society. Klee et al. (1995) comment on: 'the idealised picture of a woman who is the archetypal 'mother earth' whose life revolves around the impending birth' and the expectations of society are that 'she will be a radiant mum who is a source of support for the whole family' (p45).

Despite this widely held, idealised view, pregnancy can bring about feelings of 'loss of identity' and many women, whether drug users or not, experience pregnancy as a time of 'distress, anxiety, helplessness and isolation' (Klee et al., 1995, p45). Klee (1995) also suggests that ambivalence is a common feeling for many women during pregnancy.

Some research indicates that pregnancy can act as a catalyst for change and modification of behaviour. Neale (1999) found that for 6 per cent of the population, in her study into substitute prescribing, pregnancy featured strongly as precipitating a request for a methadone prescription (along with overdosing, leaving prison, and leaving hospital). She quotes a 21-year-old pregnant woman saying, 'I want to come off before this bairn's 'ere (pp136–7).

Siney (1995) reports that in her experience at Liverpool's Women's Hospital there was no evidence to suggest that pregnancy was, in itself, a catalyst for women to stop using drugs. She does, however, indicate that many drug using women did make changes in their lifestyle as a result of their pregnancy (p1). Drug using women who become pregnant are faced with society's stereotypes of pregnancy and the subsequent condemnation by many for not living up to these ideals: 'As a result of sexist stereotypes women drug users are viewed as doubly deviant because of disregarding and challenging their "feminine" identity' (Bates et al., 1999, p5).

There appears to be an unspoken and spoken assumption that drug using women 'have not planned their pregnancies, do not want their babies and will not be able to love and care for them as other mothers will'. (Macrory and Crosby, 1995, p3) In their research Klee et al. (1995) found that a widely held stereotype of a woman drug user was one of a 'devious manipulator, aggressive troublemaker, weak willed, victim, prostitute, unwashed, self-neglecting junky and, worst of all, someone who put her own self-gratification before the care of her children' (p45). It is often the case that women drug users who are pregnant become labelled as drug users and other aspects of their lives as pregnant women are ignored through the concentration on their drug use (Siney, 1995 and Macrory, 1997).

As a result of these stereotypes the situation for drug using pregnant women is a difficult one. Drug users themselves are subject to 'double discrimination and exclusion' (Buchanan and Young, 1997). Pregnancy for a woman who uses drugs can only add to this discrimination and exclusion. Mountenay (1999) found that pregnant women drug users often had 'early histories of poverty, violence, child abuse and family dysfunction' (p7), and women with problem drug use were found to be more likely to have the medical and social problems associated with deprivation and exclusion, along with the medical and social problems associated with drug use. She also found that 'stigmatisation relating to drug use can drive a wedge between the drug user and mainstream society' (p7). Therefore at a time when advice and medical support are vital, a pregnant woman drug user is more likely to be excluded from the service she requires to the detriment of herself and her child.

Services tailored to the needs of pregnant drug users

There have been significant changes, over the last decade, in how drug use is dealt with at a national and local level. Whilst the government's strategy *Tackling Drugs to Build a Better Britain* (1998) does not address specifically the area of pregnancy and drug use, it does set out its aims under the section on treatment to: 'ensure all the problem drug misusers, irrespective of age, gender, race, and drug with which they have a problem, have proper access to support from appropriate services, including primary care, when needed. Providing specific support services for young people, ethnic minorities, women and their babies' (p2). There was also an intention (as set out in the *Tackling Drugs Together* (1995) that drug action teams and drug reference groups would lead to a 'greater cohesion of effort and sharing of resources amongst health and local authorities, criminal justice agencies and other key players, agreed action plans and better prioritisation of local need'. *Tackling Drugs to Build a Better Britain* (1998) recognised that drug problems do not occur in isolation and the Social Exclusion Unit set up in December 1997 is looking at many of the problems often associated with drug taking such as 'school exclusions, truancy, rough sleeping and poor housing' (p1). As a socially excluded group, this may impact favourably on pregnant drug users.

Whilst these broader strategies attempt to address drug use, they do not give specific guidance in relation to pregnant women who use drugs. Whilst The Children Act 1989 does not deal specifically with drug using parents (Bates et al., 1999, p5) the principles it espouses of partnership, the importance of families, the idea of children in need and of significant harm provide the baseline for all professionals who work with children and families where substance misuse is an issue. In *Changing Childbirth: Good Practice in Maternity Care* (DOH 1993) good principles of maternity care are outlined for all pregnant women. *Working Together* (1991, 1999) stresses the importance of multi-agency liaison when working with children and families. It gives guidelines on confidentiality and information sharing in order that the child's needs may be promoted.

In 1997 the Local Government Drugs Forum and the Standing Conference on Drug Abuse published *Drug Using Parents: Policy Guidelines for Inter-agency Working*. This document recommends that 'all services should have a written ante-natal policy about drug use in pregnancy which recognises the fears and disapproval that drug using parents may face'. It also recommends that: 'all maternity services should have policies and procedures for pregnant women who use drugs and for the care of the new born infants of drug users.' (p7). These recommendations aim to encourage women into ante-natal care to receive appropriate support to stabilise, reduce or stop their drug use. Whatever the local arrangements, there is an emphasis on the need for multi-disciplinary working and the provision of all appropriate services to encourage drug using pregnant women to come forward without fear of discrimination (p 30). The document offers guidance on assessment, prescribing during pregnancy and labour, breast-feeding, HIV and hepatitis. There is advice for professionals on liasing and the setting up of multi-agency planning meetings, as well as information for pregnant drug users.

There is clear advice that a child protection case conference should not be called unless: 'there is concern about the effect of problem drug or substance use on the lifestyle and consequently on the child care abilities of a pregnant drug user' (p31). It is intended that: 'these guidelines should improve the care provided to pregnant drug using women and should ensure a consistent approach throughout the country' (Hepburn, 1999).

The Institute of The Study of Drug Dependence have recently published their *Guide for Professionals: Drugs, Pregnancy and Child Care* (Mountenay, 1999). This guide draws on the recommendations and guidelines suggested in *Drug Using Parents* (1997) whilst giving more specific information on the medical and social issues around pregnancy, child care and drug use.

Despite the guidance, the service provision available for pregnant drug users varies from one health authority to the next. Klee et al. (1998) report how services 'range from apparent absence to formalised and well developed guidelines and procedures' (p78).

The Manchester model

Some health authorities such as Manchester and Liverpool have created posts of drug liaison midwife. Growing out of experience in the voluntary sector and the identification of an increased need, the Manchester service was set up to improve the accessibility and appropriateness of maternity services for drug using women and their families. The aim in creating this post was to establish an inter-agency, collaborative, city-wide support system to improve the quality of care for this client group. Jointly employed by Central Manchester Healthcare Trust and the Mental Health Services of Salford NHS Trust since August 1995, the drug liaison midwife is responsible for leading the development of good policy and practice in the treatment and support of pregnant drug users and those who are HIV positive.

Whilst not detracting from the routine maternity services available for all pregnant women, the drug liaison midwife works on a weekly basis with MASH (Manchester Action on Street Health). This service enables women working as street prostitutes, and often unregistered with a GP, to be given ante-natal care and access to maternity services. By offering this outreach, specialist service, the midwife is able to offer advice and practical help around pregnancy and drug use at an early point. The relationship and trust established by this approach enables staff to make more focused interventions at a later stage in pregnancy, without alienating service users. The crisis interventions that previously arose when an unknown, unbooked, drug user presented in labour, are therefore avoided.

The aim is to create an ante-natal and post-natal environment where women feel free to disclose their substance use without fear of being further marginalised. Manchester has experienced an increase in the number of women disclosing drug use during their pregnancy. This may reflect the increase in drug use per se, but also reflects the increased skills of midwives in eliciting information in a sympathetic and non-judgemental manner (Macrory, 1999). In Manchester, women with problematic drug use are not admitted to the maternity services for detoxification or stabilisation, as it is considered not to be the most appropriate place to address the complex issues associated with a drug problem. Pregnant women are prioritised for individual assessments for treatment on the in-patient unit at the regional drug service hospital. However, in other areas, if no other option is available, for some women admission to the ante-natal ward may be beneficial in the short term, but only with very close involvement and supervision by the drug team/worker.

The drug liaison midwife has worked towards promoting a consistent service for drug using women. Pain for every woman is an individual, subjective experience and the requirements of opiate dependent women should be no different than other women, provided they have their methadone level maintained.

Following the birth, the mother and baby are now transferred to the ward together, unless medical reasons dictate otherwise. Should babies require treatment, they usually return to the special care baby unit. As most major symptoms of withdrawal will show after 24 hours and before 72 hours (McIvor and Shaw, 1994), a stay of 72 hours is recommended. Good liaison with the community midwifery service, the health visitor and the GP, ensures extra support once discharged home. As the automatic admission of the baby to the special care baby unit has ceased, women now have the opportunity to realistically address their drug use during pregnancy, rather than them desperately (and usually unsuccessfully) trying to be drug-free by the birth. The anxiety of knowing their babies will be separated from them, and the fear of their confidentiality being compromised, would seriously disrupt a previously stable treatment programme with the drug service. Of the last 60 babies born to drug using mothers at St Mary's Women's Hospital in Manchester only two were admitted, for the treatment of drug withdrawal, to the special care baby unit (Macrory, 1999).

In these instances the focus is on support and encouragement to help women cope with what is often a very irritable and unsettled baby. Breast-feeding is actively encouraged, and those who wish to are usually more motivated to further address their drug use. Babies are observed on the ward by the mother and the staff, using a modified score chart. The staff are encouraged to view the babies condition holistically, using the chart as a guide, rather than a subjective tool. Whilst less is obviously better, the amount and type of drug used is not a reliable indicator as to how the baby may react.

These changes in practice, since the development of the specialist service, have led to a dramatic reduction in pharmacological treatments and, in Manchester, no baby has been readmitted with problems related to withdrawal.

If an accessible, user-friendly service for staff and clients alike can be provided, the potential for stress for everyone involved in the plan of care is reduced, or removed. This contributes to the goal of providing a seamless service between the drug and maternity services, for both clients and health professionals alike.

Case history
Wendy has a six-year-old son, and was 13 weeks pregnant with her second child when first referred to the drug liaison midwife. She was stable on a

methadone programme and doing well. In her first pregnancy she had been too frightened to tell anyone about her heroin use, as she believed her baby would be taken into care if staff found out. She was also too scared to ask anyone whether her baby would be damaged as a result of her drug use.

The whole experience of her first pregnancy and the first six months of motherhood had been so dreadful that she had delayed a much-wanted pregnancy until now. Her family was completely unaware of her long-term drug use and she was extremely anxious that staff would breach confidentiality if her baby went to the special care baby unit.

Wendy was very relieved when she knew that this baby would remain with her on the ward, delighted that she could breast-feed, and that it was not automatically assumed that she would be unable to care for her child. Staff were supportive and aware of the need for confidentiality, rather than being critical of her. Wendy and the agencies involved were able to work in partnership to ensure the best outcome for her second child.

Wendy then continued with her drug reduction programme, addressing her drug use realistically, rather than desperately trying to get drug free before the birth.

The impact of tailored services

Areas where specialised services are available show more positive outcomes for the pregnant drug user and her child. Siney and Morrison (1995) comment that 'those units with more experience of seeing pregnant drug misusers are more adept at identifying such women' (p16).

The relationships between client and health professional were found to be consistently good in those clinics and hospitals in which a specific policy had been developed, and because of the multi-agency approach social work departments were involved at a much earlier stage in a supportive rather than a child protection role (Macrory, 1995). This joint approach also means that pregnant women are prioritised for treatment by the drug agencies (Klee et al., 1995).

Women's fear of disclosing drug use during pregnancy and subsequently the lack of appropriate treatment for her and the baby is still of major concern. However, we now recognise that women are far more likely to disclose their drug use if a specialist service exists (LGDF, 1997). Siney (1995) explains that by 'identifying themselves earlier in the pregnancy to a specialist service the women have more opportunity to ask questions and to allow professionals to give them choices' (p9). This inevitably has a positive impact on the newborn, with evidence from the United States cited in Siney (1995) showing that: 'illness in babies born to drug dependant women was directly related to the amount of ante-natal care they received' (p10).

By presenting earlier in pregnancy to an appropriate service, a more thorough understanding of the family's social conditions is gained, more appropriate obstetric care is available, and a more thorough assessment of family support and potential child protection issues is possible. This intervention then impacts positively on the health of the mother and the child and may lead to the prevention of a child being placed in a special care baby unit or, in some cases, being unnecessarily exposed to the risk of significant harm (Mountenay, 1999).

Evaluations of successful projects have identified gaps in service provision and barriers, which prevent women approaching the maternity services earlier on in pregnancy. As a group of women, predominantly excluded from society as a result of their lifestyle, this group face the added problem of an inconsistent and poor service during their pregnancy.

Overcoming common barriers to service provision

Staff who work in maternity services often have a varying knowledge base about substance misuse, from the limitations of moral dogma, though to more formal training. The pregnant drug user may struggle to get the consistent and correct advice that is vital to her and the baby's well-being. Many women fear that they will be separated from their newborn child, either through admission to the special care baby unit, or through admission into care following concerns about child protection issues (Macrory, 1995; Hepburn, 1997; Siney, 1995; Mountenay, 1999). This fear does have some basis in reality. In areas where a specialist service is not available, the majority of the babies are separated from their mothers and admitted to special care units, and child protection case conferences are sometimes convened. These often require babies to remain in hospital until a decision is made (Siney and Morrison, 1995, p17). This separation has a prolonged negative impact on the bonding between mother and child.

Many women drug users may already have children to care for and a busy lifestyle maintaining their own drug use. They are not likely to prioritise hospital appointments and this may act as a barrier for some. Hepburn (1999) comments that poor compliance with services is a reflection of the inappropriate nature of those services which fail to recognise the woman's lifestyle and her wide range of other problems.

Those specialist services in existence are continually developing to meet the needs of their users, and can offer advice to other areas developing their own services. This advice is generally aimed at helping women overcome barriers by providing a service with a better understanding of confidentiality issues and appropriate information exchange, better communication and co-ordination, a consistent approach to drug use issues and their impact on pregnancy and child care (Klee et al., 1998; Bates et al., 1999). Emphasis is placed on in-service training, drug awareness and provision of a needs-led service. Examples of integrated specialist services (in line with the guidance produce by SCODA and LGDF (1997) do exist and have shown positive outcomes in attracting women; have provided more appropriate care during pregnancy; have prevented more severe withdrawals in babies and have reduced the need for the separation of newborn babies from their mothers.

Only by attempting to understand women's drug use in the presence of other contributory and complex issues, can we begin to challenge and change society's attitudes and reduce the risks posed to women, their unborn and their newborn babies. By maximising their health we are able to minimise harm.

References

Barry, M., and Hallett, C. (Eds) (1998) *Social Exclusion and Social Work, Issues of Theory and Practice*, Lyme Regis: Russell House Publishing.

Bates, T., Buchanan, J., Corby, B., and Young. L. (Eds) (1999) *Drug Use, Parenting and Child Protection, Towards an Effective Inter-agency Response*, Liverpool: Liverpool ACPC.

Buchanan, J., and Young, L. (1997) *Examining the Relationship between Material Conditions, Long-term Problematic Drug Use and Social Exclusion: A New Strategy for Social Inclusion*, Lancashire, University of Central Lancashire.

Department of Health (1999) *Working Together to Safeguard Children*, London: HMSO.

The Drug Misuse Research Unit, University of Manchester and Drug Monitoring Unit, Liverpool John Moores University (1998) *Drug Misuse in the North West of England 1997.*

Hepburn, M. (1997) Horses For Courses: Developing Services for Women with Special Needs, *British Journal of Midwifery* 5, 8.

Hepburn, M. (1999) *Women and Drug Use*, Bolton Document.

Hepburn, M., and Elliot, L. (1997) A Community Obstetric Service for Women with Special Needs, *British Journal of Midwifery* 15, 8.

Howard, C. (1997) *Neonatal Withdrawal: A District Centre Experience and Review of the Literature*, unpublished research paper.

Klee, H., Lewis, S., and Jackson, M. (1995) *Illicit Drug Use, Pregnancy and Early Motherhood. An Analysis of Impediments to Effective Service Delivery*, Centre for Social Research on Health and Substance Abuse.

Klee, H., Lewis, S., and Jackson, M. (1998) *Illicit Drug use, Pregnancy and Early Motherhood*, Centre for Social Research on Health and Substance Abuse, University of Manchester.

Leopold, B., and Steffan, E. (1997) *Special Needs of Children of Drug Misusers: Final Report 1997*, Brussels, EEC.

Local Government Drugs Forum, Standing Conference on Drug Abuse (1997) *Drug Using Parents: Policy Guidelines for Inter-agency Working.*

Macrory, F. (1997) *Drug Use, Pregnancy and Care of the Newborn: A Guide for Professionals.* St Mary's Hospital for Women and Children and Manchester Drug Service.

Macrory, F., and Crosby, S. (1995) *Special Care or Segregation? The Need for Improvement in the Provision of Maternity Services for Drug Using Women.* Joint Presentation at 6th International Conference on the Reduction of Drug Related Harm.

McIvor, L., and Shaw, N.J. (1994) Neonatal Abstinence Syndrome after Maternal Methadone Treatment, *Archives of Disease in Childhood*, 71, p203.

Mountenay, J. (1999) *Drugs, Pregnancy and Child Care, a Guide for Professionals*, London: ISDD.

Priest. J., and Attawell, K. (1996) *Drugs in Conception, Pregnancy and Childbirth*. Harper Collins, London.

Siney, C. (Ed.) (1995) *The Pregnant Drug Addict*, Books for Midwives Press, London.

Siney, C., and Morrison C. (1995) Maternity Services for Drug Misusers in England and Wales: A National Survey, *Health Trends*, 27, 1.

Siney, C., Kidd, M., Walkinshaw, S., Morrison, C., and Manasse, P. (1995) Opiate Dependence in Pregnancy, *British Journal of Midwifery*, 3, 2, 69–73.

8 Therapeutic Work with Children of Substance Misusing Parents

Fiona Harbin

Introduction

This chapter is about therapeutic work, not with drug using adults, but with the children of drug using parents. It will concentrate specifically on therapeutic groupwork as a technique for this particular client group. Consideration is given to the number of children known to fall in to this client group and why the groupwork approach can be appropriate. The practical and theoretical difficulties of setting up the group are explored along with the evaluation process and plans for future developments.

Background

The setting up of the group for children of drug using parents came as a consequence of several interrelated national and local factors that were affecting our child care system. At the time, there appeared to be few, if any, services specifically aimed at the needs of this group of children. The setting up of our group was an attempt to remedy this gap in service.

Many families have the informal support systems and strategies to manage their drug use and care adequately for their children. The LGDF and SCODA indicate that: 'Most parents who use drugs are 'good enough' parents and do not neglect or abuse their children' (1997, p12).

Mountenay (1999) points out that: 'many drug users lead perfectly normal lives, some holding down a job and bringing up a family, differing little from their non-drug using peers' (p7). It is also important to note that drug use in itself is not a criterion for inclusion of a child's name on the child protection register. However, in some circumstances, parental drug use can lead to problems in the family that impact on the levels of care that children receive. Studies suggest that it is more likely that drug using families may be socially isolated, spend less time with their children and use inconsistent disciplinary methods. Parental substance misuse is also recognised as a major contributory factor in child mistreatment, particularly in child neglect (Mountenay, 1999 and Jones and Gupta, 1998).

By its very nature dependent drug use can become a time consuming and expensive way of life which may have a two-fold impact on parenting. Firstly, there may be an immediate impact on the individual's presentation and behaviour as a result of drug use. Symptoms such as drowsiness, inconsistent sleep patterns, poor mental and physical health, and withdrawal or overdose may be experienced. Secondly, there may be a more general impact on the lifestyle of the drug user. Offending behaviour to fund their drug use, association with other dependent drug users and dealers, imprisonment, possible exposure to violent situations, financial problems and housing problems, may be common place for this group of parents.

As a result of the impact of problematic drug use on the parent, the child may be affected in many ways. At a basic level a child might not have access to a warm and caring home environment, adequate clothing and nutrition. The lack of parental supervision could place the child in risky situations and possibly lead to regular accidents and accidental injuries (see Chapter 2). A child may be deprived of routine within the household, which is especially important for the development of younger children and babies. Experiencing this adult behaviour may be very distressing for a child, who might also be required to take on age inappropriate levels of practical and emotional responsibility for themselves, their siblings and even their parents. A child may experience periods of separation from their parents, some of which can be unplanned and traumatic. It is also likely that a child living with a problematic drug using parent has witnessed drug use on a regular basis and could have access to drugs and drug paraphernalia (LGDF and SCODA, 1997; Mountenay, 1999). Greif and Drechsler (1993) who worked with parents in a methadone maintenance group identified that it was common for this group to experience problems in: 'providing a daily structure, being consistent, managing their children's anger and coping with their children's transition in to adolescence' (p341).

Whilst research and practice in the field have identified these possible difficulties for families where there is problematic drug use, each family must be assessed separately and it cannot be assumed that drug use in itself is impacting on parenting without a thorough assessment of the family situation. This assessment should consider the needs of the child, any risk or evidence of significant harm for the child, the parents ability to care for their child, how the family copes with drug use, how help can be provided and how willing the parents are to accept and benefit from the help available (LGDF and SCODA, 1997). Many of these families may be socially excluded and may be experiencing a wide range of other problems. Even if the drug use alone was addressed there would not necessarily be an improvement in the overall situation. Mountenay (1999) points out that: 'The nature of the link between drug misuse and child abuse is complex, involving factors such as mental illness and poverty' (p36). Figures regionally and nationally show an increase in the prevalence of parental drug use impacting detrimentally on parenting ability. The number of people known to be using drugs is increasing, and within this the gap between the number of male and female drug users is decreasing, especially in the fifteen to twenty-five-year-old age group. (Drug Misuse in The North West of England, 1997 and Home Office, 1998). With women predominantly the primary carers of children, this disproportionate increase in the number of women users is more likely to have an impact on child care and pregnancy.

Mountenay (1999) indicates that: '30 per cent of registered addicts are women of childbearing age' (p7).

Bolton social services figures show an increase in the number of child concern enquiries regarding children living with drug using parents, and almost half of the children who are placed on the child protection register have parents who are dependent drug users. The majority of these children are registered under the category of neglect. In Bolton the number of children who are presented to the fostering and adoption panel for long-term placements away from their parents have parents who are drug users. This reflects research that shows that drug using parents are: 'likely to reject court ordered services and make service delivery difficult and therefore are likely to have their children removed permanently' (Curtis and McCullough, 1993; Tracy and Farkas, 1994; Murphy et al., 1991; in Hohman, 1998, p276).

This predominantly female group of parental drug users faces the same barriers as do all drug users in accessing services to offer support and help them address their drug use. However, Elliott and Watson (1998) in their study into the needs of drug using parents, found that: 'what being (or becoming) a parent did do was to throw some of these barriers into sharp relief' (p51). The authors explain that parents also have to face the 'stigma attached to being a drug using parent; fears about losing care and/or custody of the children; and the lack of alternative child care options available' (p3). Services are often seen as predominantly male orientated with no provision for families or child care, and there are still widely held views in society that women's drug use is less acceptable than men's (Copeland and Hall, 1992).

Within this situation there appears to be no systematic support for the children of drug using parents. The majority of specific services provided for these families, whilst often limited, are generally aimed at the adults in the family. These services may have benefits for children, but are not tailored to providing identified support for children and provide no clear understanding of children's needs or perceptions of their situation, or of their relationship to their parent's drug use. Children who live with drug using parents are exposed to society's views on drug use, as is any other child. With messages from the media that drugs can kill, drug use can spread infectious diseases and how drug use is wrong, this group of children have then to live with the knowledge of their own parents drug use. It is not surprising that these children are often confused and worried for their parents well-being and may be living with the daily fear that their mother or father may die, or be imprisoned and that they may be placed in care.

The groupwork approach

Having identified a need for a service for these children it was necessary then to decide on the most appropriate approach to meet this need. As information available suggested that there was likely to be a large number of children who were or had been living with parental drug use, it was decided that a specific children's group would be set up.

There are many advantages in providing services through a groupwork method. Group attendance can provide access to the experiences of other group members. A group can be a forum for creativity, it can often be more fun than individual work, and can reduce feelings of isolation by the knowledge that others may have had some similar experiences. The group-work approach can provide a structured setting for members to express their own concerns and feelings and it may provide a forum for diffusing the sense of shame and stigma that the children of drug using parents may feel. Through attendance the children will have the opportunity to learn that other group members have had similar experiences and this can offer: 'confirmation, affirmation, and acceptance to the child' (Kahn, 1994, p49 in Springer, Pommeroy and Johnson, 1999).

Social workers in our area reported feeling restricted in what they could offer to these children, and the possibility of groupwork was seen as a way forward. When the identified children were consulted about the proposal, they responded enthusiastically at the prospect of attending a group.

Acknowledging that individual work is an important part of supporting a young person and ascertaining the individual needs of the child, it was agreed that those attending the group would first undergo an individual assessment by their key worker. This would ensure that the facilitators would have a clear understanding of the child's own situation, their identified needs, their literacy skills and their level of understanding.

Fortunately, the establishment of groupwork for different client groups within the children and families division in Bolton SSD had been identified as an objective of the child protection unit and this particular group was prioritised due to the perceived need within the authority.

The group for children of drug using parents ran twice in 1998 and 1999. The third group started in March 2000. The groups were specifically for children who had lived with or were living with parental drug misuse.

Aims and objectives

Before considering the practicalities of setting up the group and the work that would be undertaken, clear aims and objectives were required. The background information that led to the setting up of the group had clearly indicated a need for support for this group of children and therefore the group would be therapeutic in nature. Although some information from the group would need to be shared with the key worker, the group would not form part of a formal assessment and it was not intended that the group be a forum to gather specific information about the children's family circum-stances. It was understood that each child who was referred to the group had experienced parental drug misuse and that this (and usually other parenting difficulties) had impacted in some way on the levels of care they had received. The knowledge gained about children's individual circumstan-ces was collated to gain a clearer understanding of children's experiences of parental problematic drug use and to develop more appropriate interven-tions and services for children in future.

The primary aim was for the children and young people to realise that there were others who lived with parental drug use, who may have had similar experiences to themselves. Within the group we aimed to provide a therapeutic environment in which to explore and address some of their common issues.

Seven objectives were identified:

1. To enable the young people to share, with others, their own experiences and feelings, if they chose to do so. (We understood that due to the sensitive nature of the topic, some children may have chosen not to do so. There were no expectations or direct questions.)
2. To enable the children to talk about feelings and emotions. (We began with the opportunity to think about feelings and how they affect us all, this was a safe way for the children to start thinking about their own feelings.)
3. To enable children to have access to age appropriate activities. (Some of the children may have been taking on age inappropriate responsibility. Within the group, children would be able to behave and play as children.)
4. To offer the group members age appropriate education on drug use and drugs. (We knew that all the group members would have some knowledge of drug use, but some of the information that the children held would be limited and inaccurate. The children likely to attend the group would be a group who were vulnerable to becoming dependent drug users themselves. This made the need for some drug awareness education all the more pertinent.)
5. To enable the group members to consider issues of personal care and safety. (The children attending the group were likely to be vulnerable children who were more likely to have suffered accidental injuries, abuse and impaired health and development.)
6. To enable the children to consider issues of loss and separation. (Many group members had experienced separation from one or both parents following prison sentences or family breakdown. Springer, Pomeroy and Johnson (1999) indicate that following the incarceration of a parent children may 'experience profound sadness, a sense of loss similar to death in the family, a drop in school performance, and stigma associated with the imprisonment of a family member' (p55). Many of the children referred had limited contact with one parental figure following parental separation and were living with either foster parents or extended family members. A significant minority had experienced the death of a family member.)
7. To enable the children to consider their own self-esteem and identity (Many of the children were isolated and would benefit from the opportunity to talk about themselves with an emphasis on positive aspects of their identity and background.)

These aims and objectives were appropriate whatever the age group of the children who attended. It was recognised, however, that the exercises and group activities would need to be adapted to the needs of the children who attended.

Due to the sensitive nature of the subject area, the group was to be a closed group. A set programme of activities and exercises was planned that would go at the pace of the children. The programme would however be flexible and we acknowledged that the group might have to continue beyond the planned period. By sharing the aims and objectives of the group with the carers and workers it was hoped that these themes could be reinforced outside the group.

The referral process

As a social services funded group we could only take referrals from social workers relating to children they were currently working with, or had worked with in the past. We put together a simple leaflet and a referral form and targeted social workers, residential social workers, foster parents and review and conference chairs with our publicity material. Referrals were slow to come. Groupwork was not always a priority in a busy social work department, and where workers had identified children, parental consent was not always forthcoming. Many parents were reluctant to allow their child to attend a social work run group that was specifically for the children of drug using parents. Whilst there appeared to be a fear that the group would be an opportunity to gather information about the parents, there was also a fear that some children were too young to look at issues of drug use. This concern was expressed by some foster carers and extended family carers who were apprehensive that the children would find the group disruptive and unsettling.

Reassurance was given that the group would not concentrate on the specific experiences of the individual children involved, but look generally at the issues. It was acknowledged that for some children, however, the subject matter might be distressing and in these cases the group may not be appropriate for that particular child. It was explained in the publicity that the child should want to attend and the referrer should have completed an assessment on the appropriateness of this prior to referral.

We spent some time considering what the specific criteria should be for the groups, and how the referred children could be placed together in a group with reference to age, gender, levels of understanding and personal experience.

The groupwork experience

To date two group programmes have been completed. The first consisted of six children, two boys and four girls, whose ages ranged from six to 11 years old. The second group consisted of six girls whose ages ranged from seven to nine years old. The third group began in March 2000 and is ongoing at the time of writing. This consists of four 14–16-year-old girls.

The majority of referrals were for children not living, at that time, with their parents, and consideration was given to whether it would be appropriate to have a 'mixed group' of those children living with parents and those living with alternative carers. Due to the changing circumstances of many of the children referred, it was decided that a mixed group would be the most appropriate. All the children in the first group lived with foster carers and five of the six children in the second group lived with foster carers or extended family members. Of the sixteen young people who have attended only one was living with their parent.

To ensure the children wanted to attend the group each was visited by a group facilitator and the referrer. It was explained to them why they had been invited to attend the group and information was given about the issues that would be covered. The children were encouraged to ask questions about the group, and all the children who were identified expressed a keenness to attend. The following case histories typify the experiences of many of the children who have attended the group.

Sara
Sara is 12 years old; she lives in foster care with her younger brother. Her younger sisters live in another foster placement. They have regular contact. Sara's mother has recently been released from prison. She is still a dependent heroin user and is currently living with a group of friends. Sara's mother rarely attends the contact sessions with her children and there are no plans for Sara or her siblings to return home. Sara's mother began using amphetamines on a recreational basis four years ago. Within twelve months she was dependent on heroin. She had little family support and Sara, as the oldest of the children, was caring on a daily basis for her younger siblings. The children's names were placed on the child protection register due to a variety of concerns about the home environment and the detrimental impact this was having on their lives. They were accommodated following the youngest child ingesting some tablets that were in the home and their mother being intoxicated to the point of being unable to speak coherently. Soon after their mother was sentenced to two years in prison for drugs related offences.

Sara is settled in her foster placement and presents as extremely sensible and mature for her age. She has continued to take on emotional responsibility for her siblings and finds it difficult to pass this over to their adult carers.

David
David is nine years old. He has lived with foster carers for two years following the breakdown of his placement with maternal grandparents. David's mother is a dependent heroin user. She left him in the care of her parents when he was five years old. Moving away she had no contact with her son for a year. David now has weekly unsupervised contact with his mother. They both enjoy this contact but David's mother continues to use drugs and lead a chaotic life. David accepts he cannot live with his mother,

however he regularly hits out at his foster parents in apparent frustration with his current situation.

Zoe

Zoe is eight years old. She lives with her mother and brother. Zoe's name has been on the child protection register for over two years due to concerns about the levels of care that her mother offers. Her mother is a dependent heroin user and funds this use through dealing and prostitution. There is a strong attachment between Zoe and her mother and her mother has attempted many of the treatments available to address her drug use as she recognises the impact it is having on her children. As a result of this she has had many drug free periods but has to date resumed her drug use within four months of the treatment. Zoe has a very supportive maternal grandmother who often cares for Zoe and her brother when her mother is in treatment or unable to manage. Zoe is a very quiet girl who is guarded about sharing information about herself. She presents as suspicious of others and prefers to spend time on her own.

Jane

Jane is 15 years old. She lives with her maternal aunt. For many years she cared for her younger sister, whilst her mother stayed in her bedroom, as a result of drug use and related ill health. Following several occasions when she had been left alone to care for her sister, alternative placements were found with the family's agreement. Jane is now a very confident outgoing teenager. She presents as street wise and craves independence. She chooses to see her younger sister on a fortnightly basis, but the meetings often involve Jane becoming angry and leaving.

Group facilitators

There were three group facilitators with groupwork experience in each group. However, the subject focus of these groups was a new experience for each of us. Due to the ages of the children attending and the need for adequate supervision, it was agreed that eight children per group would be the maximum. The use of three facilitators prevented the introduction of other workers to the group to cover absence. The group facilitators were all part of the planning process and agreed the main aims and objectives of the group. Time was taken to plan each session on a weekly basis and to adapt the plan, if necessary, at short notice. Time was also taken to debrief and record each group session.

Practical arrangements

The groupwork was funded by the social services department, and the staff involved were able to take time out from their daily work duties to run and plan the group. This took place in a central family centre where there was access to two group rooms, kitchen facilities and play equipment. A light meal and refreshments were provided for the children. The groups took place after school and lasted for approximately two hours, transport to and from the group was provided. Unfortunately, the group leaders were required to provide the transport, which meant that the debriefing sessions could not take place immediately after the group session. (However, the journeys to and from the group were often times when children spoke more openly about some of their own experiences.)

Finance was available for one group outing per group. This took place in the middle of the groupwork programme. These outings were chosen by the children, the first group choosing ten pin bowling, the second choosing a children's activity centre.

The programme

Ground rules

Confidentiality was a major cause of anxiety for carers and referrers and it was important that this was addressed in the group at the outset. With young children this concept is more difficult to explain. The facilitators stated in the first session of each group that the information shared in the group would not be shared outside, unless what the children said led the facilitators to believe that either a group member, or another child, was suffering harm. It was explained that the information would be shared with the person who referred them to the group or another adult who may be able to help. The facilitators clarified that this had been fully understood by the children attending.

It was agreed with the referrers that brief summaries of the child's involvement with the group would be provided when the sessions finished. Throughout both the groups there was only one occasion when information that had caused concern had to be shared with the referrer.

Other ground rules were set out and discussed with the group members. For all the groups the basic rules were the same. Along with confidentiality, it was agreed that each group member would listen to what others had to say, aggressive behaviour would not be tolerated, time out was available to all the members and there was no compulsion to take part in any of the group exercises. Both groups chose some of their own rules. These included 'not to laugh at others but to laugh with them', 'not to throw things' and 'not to go into the toilet when others were in there'. The ground rules were always on display and referred to if necessary.

Introductions

In the groups some of the children knew each other. There were two siblings in each of the first two groups, and other children were at the same school or had lived in the same neighbourhoods. This made the issue of confidentiality and information sharing more pertinent for the children attending. Simple circle exercises were used as a form of introduction. This exercise and the discussion around ground rules, with time for free play and tea, filled the first session.

Member autonomy

Occasionally, group members opted out of group exercises and this could distract the other children. The children had some level of autonomy over what was covered in the group and many of the children's own ideas were popular with the whole group. Two of the older girls in the first group devised an exercise on 'what to do if . . .' and chose situations from their own experiences for the group to discuss. They talked about finding 'drugs' and 'syringes' and discussed seeking appropriate help. These ideas were accommodated within the wider aims and objectives of the group.

In the first group three of the children, at their request, role-played a scenario of a family where drug use was causing difficulties and contrasted it with how the family managed when they were offered support. They were able to identify aspects of parenting which were inappropriate (and in one case abusive) and contrast this with a warm and caring home environment. In a group that was sometimes difficult to manage, this focussed everyone's attention for two sessions. The facilitators were able to expand on aspects of the role-play for wider group discussion. This play was videotaped and, as the group gained confidence in their identity and presentation, they requested that all activities be videotaped in future sessions.

Drug awareness

We planned that two sessions would cover this specifically, and wider issues around drug use would be discussed within the other topics on the programme. It was apparent, from the general discussion in the group, that all the children were aware of their parents drug use and had, in differing degrees, gained knowledge of this through what they had seen in their home. This differed from the view of the majority of their parents who did not think that their children were aware of their drug use.

Some of the children's memories included:

> *I remember seeing mummy through a hole in the door with a needle.*
> (Jane aged six years)

> *Mum used to go into the kitchen to take drugs, she thought I didn't know . . . yes my mum used to do that, always in the kitchen.*
> (Sue aged nine years and Amy aged seven years)

> *My mum started to take speed when I was nine years old, I told her not to . . . she started to use more, then used all the time. I saw her the other day and she's using heroin as well now. I don't think she will ever stop now.*
> (Debbie, aged 15 years)

The work on drug awareness was based broadly on the worksheets for children and young people produced by Tocade, and the 'Yakety Yak' pack (Lifeline, 1999). As an introduction to the topic the younger children drew round each other's bodies on large sheets of paper and then drew onto their bodies things that they identified as good or bad for them. The majority of the children could identify the difference between drugs from the GP that were to help them if they were unwell and drugs that were not given by the GP. The children talked about 'needle drugs' and 'injecting drugs'. Some of them knew the names of drugs such as heroin. This exercise also included discussion on substances such as tobacco and alcohol. The older group used a quiz as the basis of discussion on drug use issues. Using the body outlines as an aid to discussion, some of the older members of the groups went on to talk more specifically about drugs. One of the older children in the group had recently done a project at school on drug use and was able to share this with the group. This older group went on to look at some factual information about different drugs and the social context of drug use. Discussion was encouraged with printed cards detailing different scenarios. The young people would pick a card with a question on it such as 'what would you do if you were offered a cigarette?' or 'where do drugs come from?' The cards encouraged discussion and those with better reading skills aided others in reading these out.

Identity, self-esteem, and safety issues
These were covered in activity based sessions using games and videos. During these sessions photographs were taken of all the children whilst they took part in the activities. These were displayed on the wall during future sessions and the children were always keen, as part of their routine on arrival at the centre, to look at the new photographs displayed. Both groups enjoyed putting together videos of role-play scenarios, even the most reticent of group members took part in dressing up and acting. The more confident members of each group encouraged the others and all expressed pride in their achievements. The second group was enthusiastic to invite their parents and carers to watch the video that they had made. This promoted discussion of the role-play topics and built on the confidence that was developing in the groups. This also encouraged carers to continue the themes of the group at home.

Games were played that encouraged the children to say positive things about themselves and other group members. It was noticeable that many of the children were unable to make positive statements about themselves, but, without prompting, other group members suggested positive attributes and this appeared to promote positive group relationships.

Through 'feelings faces' the children spoke about the expressions on the cut-out faces and the feelings that these represented. The children were encouraged to indicate their moods on their own 'feelings face' at the beginning and end of each session. Some were reluctant to do this on occasions.

Some age appropriate educational videos were used on issues of personal safety. A minority of the children had seen these before and did not want to watch them. The videos led in to a discussion about safety and again printed cards were used to introduce scenarios for the children to consider the most appropriate response.

The children all enjoyed modelling objects from clay and other sensory play. They appeared to appreciate the sensory aspect of the activity rather than just finishing the models. During this activity some of the older group members aided the younger ones.

Loss and bereavement
This was covered in many of the sessions, when children shared their own experiences in group discussions. Issues around death came out during the role-plays to do with drug use and its social context. The two plays made up by the second group involved people dying or collapsing after being given drugs by another person. This was discussed in the groups and it was apparent that these were the experiences of many of the children relating to drug use.

Eating together
Eating together was seen as an important group activity but was not always an easy situation to manage. The first group was often preoccupied with the meal provided, asking on arrival at the centre what this was going to be and what time it would be served. The food was usually a light snack and the children initially helped themselves from the table. This became difficult to manage as the children tended to put more food than they could eat on their plates, leaving less for other group members. This led to arguments amongst the group. After several sessions the food was always provided on the plates for the children and the situation eased. This group of children all lived in foster care and there was no reason to believe that there was not enough food at home. However, many of the children, whilst living with their parents, had not always had adequate food and this behaviour was possibly an indication of this.

Managing group behaviour
It was apparent, after two sessions of the first group, that the differences in ages (from 6–11 years) meant that the ability and behaviour of group members was very varied. The shorter concentration levels of the younger children led to exercises and discussions being interrupted. The older members appeared frustrated by this and their behaviour on occasions mirrored that of the younger ones. By the third session it had become almost impossible to engage the children in any group activities, noise levels were high and some members began to exhibit aggressive behaviour towards others in the group and the facilitators. At one point the group did not feel a safe place for the young people, even though all the children were reported to be settled in their placements, and none were presenting behaviour that was difficult to manage.

After consultation with colleagues outside the group and lengthy discussions about whether the group should continue, it was agreed that the group would be split into two smaller groups for the exercises, with the children coming together to eat and play. With this new approach there was an immediate improvement in the behaviour and participation of the children. The second group was much closer in age and understanding and there was not the same need to divide the group, although some activities were carried out in smaller groups with feedback to the whole group.

The children appeared to benefit from the sessions being structured. There was always a drink on arrival and some free play. This was followed by a group exercise that usually lasted no more than half an hour. Following tea there would be a more general discussion relating to the activity and a short period of free play before the children left.

All the group members were given a box for the work they had done and in this was a large plain paper sketchbook that they were encouraged to use each week. The second group regularly used their free play time to make cards for each other, their mothers and the group facilitators, whereas the first group generally played with the toys in the centre.

Evaluation

The evaluation of the groups was threefold, taking into account the views of the children, their carers or parents and the key workers. The children were encouraged to take it in turns to interview each other, on video, about different aspects of the group. Following a general questionnaire, which was provided by the facilitators, they asked each other simple questions on the topics covered in the sessions.

The answers from these evaluations varied, with none of the children giving very detailed answers. Many of the children in the first group identified the food as the thing they had enjoyed the most, along with the outing. The second group, who had engaged well in the activities, identified that they had enjoyed these in the group. Some commented that they would have liked to talk more about drugs. The majority of the children commented that they would like to continue with their attendance.

For the first group a follow-up group was held a month later. This was not a structured session but the children were able to watch the video of their interviews. The second group chose to invite their carers and parents to the follow-up group, where the children put on a brief presentation about the group activities and all those present watched the videotaped role-plays and interviews. Some carers attended and the mother of one of the group members was enthusiastic about the activities that her daughter had been involved with.

The carers were asked to complete a questionnaire about what they thought the impact of the group had been on the children (some of these were not completed). Some commented that they had seen no change in their child's behaviour as a result of attending the group, some commented that their child had spoken at home about drug use issues and there appeared to be a general view that the children had enjoyed attending the groups.

The feedback from the children's social workers was positive. They found that the children had been able to talk more about their own experiences. One social worker commented that during a prison visit to her father one seven-year-old had told her father that she was 'now able to talk about drugs and that it wasn't a secret any more'.

Careful consideration was given to the evaluation of the groups by the facilitators. The evaluation of the first group led to changes in the planning of the second group. In the second group, having children closer in age appeared to have a positive impact on the cohesion of the group and their levels of engagement. Whilst there was still a difference in the levels of understanding of each of the children, this was more easily accommodated in the larger group setting.

Conclusion

In keeping with the original aims of the group, all involved children were now aware that there were others who were living, or had lived, with parental drug misuse. We hope that this knowledge helps children to feel less isolated. The children all had the opportunity to talk about their own experience of parental drug use and their feelings on this issue. The other aims were achieved, to a varying degree, by different children in the group. Whilst all of them had continued to attend, some had engaged more in the exercises than others. For some of the girls in the second group, more specific work would have been appreciated but this was not possible due to the distractions of other group members. For these children further work in a group or individual setting may have been helpful.

Working with a group of such young children was not always easy. Some of the difficulties in managing the group hindered the full exploration of the planned topics and it was felt that some of the aims were over ambitious within the structure available.

For the group to succeed it was vital that a thorough assessment of the child was undertaken beforehand and that further individual work arising from the topics discussed in the group should be available if required.

To date, the groups have only attracted one young person living with their parent. Whilst for many reasons this could be seen as understandable, the group had initially been set up to provide support to this group of children. With the many pressures on parents who use drugs, it may be unrealistic to expect them to welcome a group run by the social services department. With this in mind, we hope that a less structured, community-based, drop-in group will be made available to those children still living with their parents. This group is likely to be run by an agency other than social services. However, there is still much value in structured therapeutic groupwork for the children of drug using parents and we will continue to develop this service.

References

The Drug Misuse Research Unit, University of Manchester and Drug Monitoring Unit, Liverpool John Moores University (1998) *Drug Misuse in the North West of England 1997.*

Elliott, E., and Watson, A. (1998) *Fit to be a Parent, The Needs of Drug Using Parents in Salford and Trafford,* Public Health Research and Resource Centre and the University of Salford.

Greif, G.L., and Drechsler, M. (1993) Common Issues for Parents in a Methadone Maintenance Group, *Journal of Substance Abuse Treatment,* 14, 339–43.

Hohman, M.M. (1998) Motivational Interviewing: An Intervention Tool for Child Welfare Case Workers Working with Substance Abusing Parents. *Child Welfare,* LXXVII.

Jones, J., and Gupta, A. (1998) The Context of Decision Making in Cases of Child Neglect, *Child Abuse Review,* 7, 97–110.

Local Government Drugs Forum and Standing Conference on Drug Abuse (1997) *Drug Using Parents, Policy Guidelines for Inter-agency Working.*

Mountenay, J. (1999) *Drugs, Pregnancy and Child Care, a Guide for Professionals,* London: ISDD.

Springer, D., Pomeroy, E., and Johnson, T. (1999) A Group Intervention for Children of Incarcerated Parents: Initial Blunders and Subsequent Solutions, *Groupwork,* 11(1), 54–70.

9 Solution Focused Brief Therapy Used in a Substance Misuse Setting

Pauline Watts

Alcohol related problems do not develop in isolation. Instead people drink and develop alcohol problems in contexts and the most important of these contexts is often the family. (Velleman, 1993).

Most people have things that they find more pleasant to remember, as well as things that are more difficult, or even painful to remember. Taking note of the positive, or the less troubling experiences, or aspects of one's life, can help counter balance the effects of confronting troubling experiences problems. (Dolan, 1998).

'There is no problem that Solution Focused Brief Therapy can't resolve' Harvey Ratner explained in a presentation to first-year family therapy students in 1989. This was a field rich in invention and intervention, but to hear such convinced practitioners as Ratner, Iveson and George (George et al., 1990) made a significant difference to me in my choice of therapeutic direction. The writings of O'Hanlon (1987) and de Shazer (1985 and 1986) were followed by a stream of exciting ideas from Australia (White, 1989; Epston and White, 1990; and Durrant, 1985 and 1989) on externalising the problem, the use of narrative therapy and the importance of language.

Systemic and family therapy is based on the concept that a person's behaviour is part of a system of behaviours, which are continually interacting with each other. Change one small part of that behaviour and the rest of the system must make changes to accommodate the changed behaviour (Burnham, 1986). The problem itself is seen as having a function in maintaining the behaviours of the people in the system. In the field of addictions, this means that if someone stops using their substance of choice that doesn't necessarily mean that the rest of their lives will be problem free. Families frequently encounter problems adapting to the changed behaviour patterns. They find that their own roles and functions in the family are also changed. How they adapt or do not adapt can result in them actively sabotaging the changed behaviour or finding that they can no longer cope with their changing roles in the new system. Some families and partners do indeed manage the transition and much work with families is to help them to do this.

SFBT (Solution Focused Brief Therapy) came out of the work of de Shazer in the 1980s (de Shazer, 1988; de Shazer et al., 1986). He noticed that clients were coming into therapy having already started to solve the problems for which they were referred. This was expanded by de Shazer and Berg (Berg and de Shazer, 1993) at the Brief Family Therapy Centre in Milwaukee. Solution Focused Therapy views the change process as inevitable and constantly occurring. Therefore, close attention needs to be paid to exceptions to the problem, as this is seen as a change in the stability of the problem state and as the beginning of its end. Consequently, exceptions to problematic interactions are explored and enlarged.

SFBT also sees clients as being competent human beings, capable of looking at their lives and finding their own solutions to their problems. Erickson recounts his experience of finding a rider-less horse, which he did not recognise. Erickson rode it back to its farm, confident that the horse would know the right direction and that his own task was simply to keep the horse 'on track'. When he arrived at the farm, the horse's owners were shocked, he had just ridden a supposedly un-rideable horse home.

Clearly having a belief in competency enables the client to behave competently and surprise themselves and the therapist with previously unresourced behaviour. Just keeping them 'on track' may therapeutically be enough. Consequently, we are always looking for clients' skills, strengths and resources to tap into.

Prior to engaging families in these sessions we inform them about how we run the sessions by enclosing an information sheet with the appointment. We have a clear confidentiality statement, set out in writing on first contact with the service and again verbally when the client attends for assessment.

Our questions are based around the following themes:

- *Pre-session change*: Change that is already taking place.
- *Problem free talk*: Finding the clients skills, strengths and resources.
- *Exception finding*: Finding the chinks in the problem's armour.
- *Goal setting*: Using the miracle question will enable the client and individual family members' to vocalise their own goals.
- *Scaling questions*: If the miracle is ten and the worst that things have been is 0, where are you now on a scale of 0–10? This is a concrete measure of progress for client and therapist.

Our process with clients can follow the following path:

- *Locating resources, building on strengths*: Tapping in to knowledge previously gained of the client's skills, strengths and resources.
- *Coping*: What is the client already doing that is helpful?
- *Stopping things getting worse/back on the right track*: This is a very useful stage in addiction work when dealing with lapse and relapse.
- *View of self*: Helping clients to see themselves as agents of self-change.
- *Solution focused feedback and tasks*: The team feed back positives to the client via the therapist; and offers tasks to the client often about 'noticing'.

- *Follow-up sessions*: Are usually about change and difference and revisiting the scaling questions.
- *Finishing*: If changes have happened, confidence scaling questions can give the team, client and family an idea how the changes are going to be maintained.
- *Letters*: Sessions are followed up by a letter, feeding back the positives of the session or motivational issues (Allen, 1996). This is particularly useful with this client group where memory recall is often poor.

Timing
Maintaining a boundary of time in each session, puts the focus part into Solution Brief Therapy.

- What would be most useful to get out of the time we have got today?
- We only have ten minutes left, how can we use that usefully?
- As you have arrived late, we have only got twenty minutes, how can we best use that time?

Change
Change in Solution Focused Brief Therapy can mean very small changes indeed. It may mean getting the client to say what small change is possible and achievable between now and the next session that can move them up half a point on their scaling. The scaling questions monitor change for the client and the therapist. Achievement is often measured in very small steps.

Family work in a drug and alcohol agency
Working in the substance field in 1993 meant working on a one-to-one basis. There were pockets of practice where family intervention was seen as the norm rather than the exception, particularly Van Loo, working in Folkestone using Milan Systemic and Yandoli working in London using Solution Focused Brief Therapy. However, in my continuing training, I became intrigued with the concept of client competence and giving responsibility to the client for the outcome of therapy. Berg and Miller (1992) reinforced these ideas and offered a clear working model for using Solution Focused Brief Therapy in the field of addictions.

Clients in the drug and alcohol field, as their addiction takes over, give responsibility for managing their lives to anyone else who will take it on. This can include their family; other professionals involved (i.e. general practitioners, psychiatrists, social workers, probation officers) and their drug and alcohol counsellors. It is an easy pit in which to fall. Unfortunately, this then sets up the client as incompetent and unable to find their own solutions, or make their own decisions. Solution Focused Brief Therapy reawakens these competencies in clients and in their families.

As our team has grown, we have been able to train all the team members, using the training provided by the Brief Therapy Practice in London. In our multi-disciplinary team, the addition of this form of systemic therapy (on top of existing counselling skills) has proved a popular, enjoyable and valued addition to our team members. Without the full support of the team, any use of this form of therapy would be very difficult to implement. We have discovered that working as two teams, split into drug and alcohol specialisms, seems to fit the different dynamics which present in families. Drug clients frequently choose to be seen with their parents, while alcohol clients are mostly seen with their partners and children.

Family dynamics in addicted families

Over time families develop roles and functions that enable them to survive and cope with having an addicted person in the family. Families, as systems, adjust and accommodate the changes that addiction brings. They are 'doing' change all of the time. Life events like marriage, birth, adolescence, leaving home and death all require readjustment, as does just the passage of time and the continual impact of other systems on the family system. When a member of the family develops an addiction, the family adjusts to the addiction and accommodates it into the system. Unfortunately, some of the coping behaviours developed by family members continue to reinforce and maintain the addiction. (McGoldrick and Gerson, 1985; Velleman, 1995)

Frequently, the addiction serves a purpose in maintaining family stability. Remove the addiction and the unmentioned fear of the family is that it will fall apart. With young drug users, the phenomenon of triangulation has been observed. In this the child's drug use keeps the parental couple locked together despite poor marital functioning. Those adolescents who enter a drug culture, achieve a separation from their parents, which is not a true separation. The adolescent frequently remains locked within the family. Schoor and Beach (1993) have described this as pseudo independence.

Therefore, while the family may protest loudly about the misery of addiction, giving up their roles in this and accepting a temporarily unbalanced and addiction-free family while developing new roles, may be too difficult for them to deal with. This would result in the family members having to address underlying issues that remain unresolved all the time that an addiction exists.

Partners and families have frequently sabotaged sobriety. Some of this behaviour is subtle, or unconscious, where a situation is engineered where relapse is highly likely. Sometimes though, the drinker is given a more blatant invitation to drink, despite the family/partner taking the high moral ground and being the injured party when relapse occurs.

I see this pattern particularly with my female clients, a high proportion of whom have been sexually abused (Swett and Halpert, 1994). Research by Spak et al. (1997) discovered that the strongest predictor for a woman to develop an alcohol problem was childhood sexual abuse. High on the list, for these women, of the benefits of using alcohol, is that it enables them to participate in a sexual relationship with their partners. Take alcohol away and their sexual relationship suddenly has to be dealt with. Sometimes these women are involved with partners whose sexual practises would not normally be acceptable to them when sober. They are often abusive and based on an imbalance of power (Long and Mullen, 1994). While we would refer on for sex therapy, the woman's continued sobriety and increase in self-esteem may preclude her from continuing in the relationship. Many marriages that have been based around a substance misusing partner can often break up following abstinence for this and other reasons. Consequently, if family work is not undertaken the likelihood of relapse increases.

A volume of research now exists on the difficulties children may experience in families where a parent, or parents, are misusing drugs or alcohol (Stafford, 1992; Laybourn, Brown and Hill, 1996; Zeitlin, 1994; Woodside, 1988 and Cuijpers et al., 1999).

In 1997, Alcohol Concern and Childline published important research (Brisby et al., 1997 and Housten et al., 1997) relating to the unseen problems of these children, which are largely ignored by children's services planners. We know that between 40 per cent and 60 per cent of adults attending drug and alcohol clinics are themselves children of alcohol misusing parents (Stafford, 1992).

As a team we are very aware of children's difficulties in coping with the vagaries of addiction in the family. Seeing the family in SFBT gives the children a chance to have their say. Yes they are loyal and often guarded, but the style of therapy is relaxed, non-judgemental and often fun! Where else are they going to be asked about miracles! With very small children, we may ask them to make drawings, then tell us a story about their drawings. It never ceases to surprise us that, despite videotaping sessions and having a team behind a screen, we get so much out of our families and the children in those families. We have also found that the children can be very articulate and perceptive about their parents and substance misuse. Most children from an early age are very aware of the role substance plays in their parents' lives.

Here are examples of two families tackling the miracle question.

Example 1
Our client is a 48-year-old mother, Angie. This is her 12-year-old son from her first marriage, Carl. Four years ago, her two sons from that marriage, then eight and twelve, were removed from her care by social services because of her chaotic opiate and alcohol misuse and lack of care and control of the children. The children were subsequently returned to their father. Recently, her younger son moved back in with her, after revealing to his GP that his father was hitting him and being emotionally abusive. We were concerned that the mothers' current level of substance misuse and her accommodation and lifestyle did not provide a secure and stable environment. Carl brought in some Lego and played with it throughout. He was quite difficult to engage until we asked this miracle question.

TH: I am going to ask a funny sort of question, but it might help you see more clearly what you both want. I will ask you both separately. Angie you may have heard it before. You go home from here and tonight you go to bed and go to sleep. While you're asleep a miracle happens, but because you're asleep, you don't know that a miracle has happened, but when you wake up in the morning things will be different, because a miracle has happened. What would you notice that tells you a miracle has happened? What would you see? What would be different?

Carl: Well my mum and dad wouldn't be here, because they are what made me.

TH: Mum and dad wouldn't be here?

Angie: (Laughter)

TH: They are what made you?

Carl: They are what made me. You said, took away the problems that made you, problems that brought you here today.

TH: So mum and dad are the problems that brought you here today?

Carl: Not the problems but . . .

TH: What else would you notice that was different?

Carl: Well . . . what do you mean by today. Is it like today and they go off?

TH: Say . . . imagine you sleep, something happens, something dramatic and miraculous which transforms your life, takes away the problems that brought you here.

Angie: Makes your life perfect.

TH: Wouldn't necessarily say perfect, but takes away the problems that brought you here.

Carl: A few pounds would sort me out nicely.

Angie: (Explosive laughter).

TH: So it's just lack of money?

Carl: Not enough time in the day for having fun.

TH: Anything else? You were saying earlier on that your mum and dad wouldn't be in the picture. I was wondering if that was serious or not?

Carl: I wouldn't want them to go away, but you said what problems had brought me here today?

TH: So mum and dad are sort of a key to that?

Silence.

Question from the team: what are the problems that your mum and dad make for you?

Carl: They make rules for themselves. Make me do jobs. Not letting me spray paint in the house. (Laughs).

Angie: Carl's ideal world would be to have us both living together again.

TH: Is that your ideal world Carl?

Carl: Nods in the negative.

Angie: I asked you where you wanted to live yesterday and you said with both of you.

TH: So what do you mean by that Carl?

Carl: Both in the same house but not together, then sometimes I could be with my mum *and* my dad.

TH: So you like being with your mum and dad but not at the same time. Why is that?

Carl: Because sometimes they argue.

TH: Does that upset you?

Carl: Na, it's just a bit boring. After they finish fighting they start complimenting each other.

Carl went on to reveal living in a chaotic household where other substance users came and went and where his mother was often intoxicated. He also spoke about experiencing bullying at school because he often had to defend his mothers' behaviour. He got into fights and had been excluded from school. Part of the mothers' miracle was that her son would not get into trouble, but up until now she was unable to make any link between her substance behaviour and his behaviour. He had little help or support from the school regarding the bullying.

We referred this family on to Child Psychology Service for further family intervention. We also made our concerns known to social services. We talked to the mother about how she could take up the issue of bullying at the school. We continued to support the mother on a one-to-one basis.

Example 2

This second family consists of Les, husband of Jenny and father of Dean. Les went into an alcohol treatment centre two years previously. He then spent time in a dry house and then his own flat. He had got back with his family six months before this session. He had contacted us because he had returned to problematic drinking and wanted to stop things getting worse. The beginning of the session was checking out how things were with them. What was the present drinking like and how was it affecting them individually.

TH: Right, well we've got a funny sort of question that we like to ask. It's called the Miracle Question. If you left here today and went home, you went to sleep tonight and a miracle happened while you were asleep, so you didn't know the miracle had happened and when you woke up in the morning all the problems that brought you here today had disappeared. What would life be like? What would you be doing?

Dean: Hmm, probably everything I've always wanted, dad's always wanted, what would probably happen, if that happened? Mmm. Then his mum and dad might send me down some stuff for my birthday, Christmas, send him something for once, cos although they get him a card . . . obviously stop the drinking.

TH: What would you be doing? What would be different to what you're doing now?

Dean: Well, if that happened, doing everything I wanted to, getting into another football team seeing if 1 could become a professional.

TH: How would dad not drinking help that?

Dean: Well, mmm, what used to happen Sunday mornings, if dad was drinking in the pub or mum was in church, cos no one could take me, so I couldn't go to the matches, even though I was good enough to get in the team, I couldn't go. If all that stopped I would probably be in the team and it would just be good to have my mum and dad by my side, cheering me on.

TH: Right

Dean: Once my dad cheered me on cos I beat this player up: he tripped me up and dad walked me down there. Mum said it must have been amazing that I played at all, because me and my dad walked to R . . ., played the game and walked all the way back!

Let's check out with mum and dad what their miracles would be.

Jenny: Well, for me, the trust would comeback. When he was not drinking, although he wasn't living with me, I could trust everything he told me. Even now . . . has he? Is he telling me the truth?

TH: What would you see yourselves doing?

Jenny: Well, he'd have a job we'd be like a normal couple, he'd go to work! and come home. That would be enough for me.

TH: Right . . . OK . . . Les?

Les: Getting on to this one. I'd be paranoid someone handing me a miracle on a plate, something gone wrong, someone's going to burst this bubble pretty soon.

TH: So you wouldn't believe it, you'd be sceptical and that would be based on your previous experience? That would be very understandable.

Les: Yeah, it's.

TH: That's being about . . . being about wise learning from experience. Let's say before someone sticks a pin in this bubble what would this bubble consist of?

Les: Just literally, me inside this bubble. Just like a big transparent football, me own space, all of a sudden everything's around me is just calm and sweet and everyone's happy.

TH: Right, so you'd be calm and happy. They would give you some space.

Les: Yeah, that's the frightening bit, I've got my own space, but it seems every one wants to come into mine. It's frightening, how close do people have to get before I push them away again. That's the way I actually feel about it though. It's bizarre. I can't take anybody on, nobody's ever been in that close. They might have done once, I think, now it's gone again. So I'm not willing to take the risk, making somebody happy, something going to go wrong again, they'll get upset again and that's it. I think, oh well it's easier to keep them at arm 's length and play it from there really.

As there did not appear to be too many problems for Carl, and his mother was a very capable carer, we continued to work with Les, and felt no need to discuss this case with social services.

Unique outcomes are those that the therapist believes clearly facilitate, for those persons who seek therapy, the re-authoring of lives according to preferred stories and are developments that might not have been exactly or generally predicted by the therapist. These unique outcomes constitute the more sparkling events of the interview.(Epston and White, 1989–91).

Often clients come up with a solution to the problem, or a unique outcome, which defies the accepted wisdom, but nevertheless works for them. I am reminded of a client whose wife decided to breathalyse him every night. He agreed to this and harboured no resentment. Although our whole team was unhappy with the solution, we encouraged them to continue because this was their chosen path. When we saw them again after six months, we were pleased to find out that his enforced abstinence had made him cope with situations alcohol free that previously he had never managed. This had given him confidence and there were times when he was on business away from home or his wife was too tired to breathalyse him, yet he maintained his sobriety because he wanted to. He had learnt to cope with situations alcohol free. She had also developed confidence in him and was learning to trust him.

When we scaled confidence early in our work with them, his wife had only managed one on the scale of 0–10. When we re-scaled in the last session, she scaled an 8–9. As her confidence was an important issue for this couple and an indicator to the team as to how well things were going for them; it also gave the team confidence to discharge them.

The key words to describe the essentials of this therapy would be competency, responsibility and client goals (not therapist goals). All of these things make it very attractive to those working in the field of addictions. Frequently we come across clients who are seen as incompetent and unable to manage even the smallest parts of their lives. A decline into addiction has meant that others around them have picked up their responsibilities. Their families cope by eventually doing everything for them.

As one person said: 'I'm expecting my third child, but I already have a third child, him (points to her husband) and I'm not prepared to put up with a fourth, I'd rather manage three children without him'. She told him that she wanted a responsible adult to co-parent with her or she would leave him. Working with SFBT we could put him back in touch with his responsible self and his coping abilities.

It often comes as a shock to clients that we expect them to have competencies and use them. We don't see addictions as an illness, but as a learnt behaviour, which can be unlearnt. Our expectation is that clients will manage that over a period of time. This expectation of a successful outcome is another very important factor in helping the client to believe in themselves (as with Milton Erickson and his horse).

Many of our clients have led largely productive lives, many still have homes and families. They have struggled to bring up children and many have managed to acquire qualifications and hold down responsible jobs. Those who are younger have often coped with a traumatic childhood and upbringing. We will be looking for the personal resources that helped them to cope with that. When their addiction develops, they and their families lose sight of those achievements. We re-engage those competencies through SFBT.

In this respect the problem-free talk at the beginning of the session is extremely important. This is not merely the 'social' stage of 'getting to know you'; we are specifically interested in successful areas of clients' lives, at home, work, school and elsewhere. We can then limit the problem-talk by referring to previously described strengths to indicate our belief that change is within the clients' control and to guide them to talking about 'exceptions'.   (George et al., 1990).

Even the most improbable client situation can produce competencies. I'm reminded of a couple that had been married for fifteen years. The husband had been out of work and drinking problematically for much of that time. They had three quite young children. So determined were they that no one should be aware of the problem, they had maintained a facade of coping, even in front of close relatives. The house was immaculate, they made appointments, attended school functions and showed a great deal of care around their children. They attempted to give the children a loving, emotionally secure and rewarding childhood (something the husband had never experienced himself). He only presented for treatment because the careful balancing and juggling act, which he and his wife had managed up until now, was starting to come apart. His wife could no longer cope with the strain. He said that his drinking was starting to affect the children's behaviour and he couldn't be the parent he wanted to be. The family income was no longer covering his, by now, extensive drinking and the growing demands of his young family. He wanted to stop drinking and get a job. We looked at what had got them through the last fifteen years, what were their strengths developed during that time, that they could now apply to managing his sobriety.

Clients also come to us having been 'told' how they should sort out their addiction by other agencies, professionals and families, often with no thought given to the clients own beliefs, gender, race or ethnicity. Recently, a client came with his wife, daughter and son-in-law. All were miserable and upset. Eighteen months previously, he had attended a rigidly interpreted rehabilitation programme, with a religious emphasis. He had relapsed, felt guilty and a failure and more importantly, his family saw him as a failure too. He was convinced, having listened to others, that he had to find his 'higher power' and that he would then manage abstinence. He then said, 'It's so difficult, particularly as I'm an atheist'. With this knowledge he was able to look at the strength of his decision-making around that belief and look at his competency to make other decisions and take control.

We discussed, with them, our way of looking at addictions as a learnt behaviour. We also explained the role of lapse and relapse, being part of a continuum of learning not to drink (di Clemente and Prochaska, 1992). All this was news to him and his family. There was a visible lifting of weight after we had explained it all. He hadn't failed, his progress towards abstinence was entirely normal, his guilt was lifted. Given that this man's drinking was initiated by guilt, the mode of treatment offered only succeeded in increasing his guilt and therefore his likelihood to drink.

I mention respect, also at this point, because it was certainly an issue with this man's partner. Too many professionals show scant respect and regard for our clients. As my client's partner said, 'We went to see X. Usually, he's very nice to me, but when he saw my husband, he was very curt and spoke to him very rudely. The look he gave him! He showed him no respect. After all this man is my husband, the father of my children. His attitude showed disrespect to me, too.'

The team felt that it was beneficial that her husband heard her say this. SFBT is respectful therapy. It is non-judgemental and doesn't presume to have any of the answers. Those are for the clients to arrive at themselves.

Using motivational interviewing with solution focused brief therapy

Using families as a motivational tool is another significant factor in their engagement. What continually surprises us is the similarity between the concepts of SFBT and Motivational Interviewing (Miller and Rollnick, 1992). Motivational Interviewing uses negative aspects of addiction to move clients through the cycle of change (Prochaska and di Clemente, 1992) and SFBT emphasises and builds on the positive. By looking at the five basic principles of Motivational Interviewing and starring those statements which particularly apply to SFBT, we can understand the high degree of overlap and the ease with which these two therapies can work together:

1. *express empathy*
   acceptance facilitates change
   skilful reflective listening
2. *deploy discrepancy*
   build awareness of consequences of different behaviours
   discrepancy between present behaviour and important goals
3. *avoid argumentation*
   arguments are counterproductive
   defending breeds defensiveness
   resistance is a signal to change strategies
   labelling is unnecessary
4. *roll with resistance*
   new perspectives are invited but not imposed
   the client is a valuable resource in finding solutions to problems
   the client should present arguments for change
5. *support self efficacy*
   belief in the possibility of change is an important motivation
   self-efficacy is not the same as self-esteem

The client is responsible for choosing and carrying out personal change. (Miller and Rollnick, 1992)

Because SFBT is a co-operative therapy, number 3 (avoid argumentation) should not arise. When someone is faced with how the negative consequences of their addiction are affecting their family (particularly their children) this provides a huge motivational impetus to change.

Here is another sequence from family 2. The therapist has been checking out with the client what his drinking has been like. Then she turns to the client's wife:

TH: To Jenny. What's the situation like for you at the moment?

Jenny: It's like I've gone back in time, like it was, you know, years ago or something and everything that's gone with it. He's not drinking to excess like he used to, he's not getting drunk every day, but there's still the money that's getting spent in the pub even though he's got a slate, he's got to pay it back at some point and then there's the lies and deceit that came with it, you know, and then I found out that when I go to work he'd go out and get back before I came back.

TH: What do you notice, Dean when he's drinking?

Dean: Often when he's just sitting down watching TV he's drinking. Come home go to the fridge for a lemonade and notice four cans and stuff, small part of the fridge is turned into a pub, every time I go there there's three, then there's four, when I come home from school there's three and it goes on like that.

TH: So you're counting?

(Hesitates, unsure).

Dean: Not counting . . . also I'm wondering if I come back and my dad's alive with his heart problem tablets.

TH: So he's taking tablets as well?

Dean: Ooh well, he's supposed to be, for his heart and any beer at any time could kill.

TH: So you're worried about that?

Dean: Yeah.

TH: Who do you talk to about it?

Dean: Well I did talk to Warren (CPN Child and Adolescent Services) about it. Until I stopped going. He also used to come to my old school, as well, he's left now.

TH: So have you got anyone to talk to now about how you feel about things?

Dean: Well I can now have the odd occasional word with Barry, he lives in Wales.

TH: Who's Barry?

Dean: Friend of dad's from rehab. He says if dad gets too out of hand just talk to him. But he works, he's not always there. We often go up there and see him. In the summer holidays. Did we go up there this year? (to dad).

Les: No.

Dean: No, we didn't have enough money this year so we didn't see him. Cos dad hasn't got many friends, doesn't get out and see people.

TH: When dad wasn't drinking what was life like for you?

Dean: Mm, it was good. The only bad bit about it was he was in B . . . and I couldn't see him very much. I can still remember the bad times when dad was drinking heavily, there was something I can't forget, get out of my mind. I asked dad to go and get me a cake or something, I think he was drunk or something, I think, lost the plate and it cracked and I was sitting in bed. I don't know how old I was . . .

The first part of this gives the team a view of how the family is functioning around the alcohol. Are things dangerous in this household? Is there neglect? Is the situation damaging for the child? Then the therapist can balance things up with life without alcohol. This is not only a good motivational tool, but also reawakens competencies and a view of a desirable goal.

TH: But recently your dad was talking about sitting in the chair and not drinking and how difficult it was, I wonder what it was like for you to have your dad at home and not drinking; that was this year?

Jenny: (To Les). You came back in February, that's when you left the flat. (To therapist). He hasn't really gone. (To Les). You've only gone a few days not drinking: most days you've had a can.

Dean: When he wasn't drinking and he was at home there was a bit more money and things had been excellent.

TH: What was so excellent about it?

Dean: Everything. My dad's not drinking, he's able to do stuff with me.

TH: What stuff did you do?

Dean: He played board games. Went into W . . . with me.

TH: So there were good times.

Dean: Yeah, we both enjoy the same TV programmes, like the Simpsons and Shooting Stars.

TH: And the arguments between you and your mum, have they stopped? Are they better?

Dean: Yeah, much better, cos what used to happen, say like if we were sitting here now, there'd be an argument. Mum would slam the door, then dad would go upstairs and slam another door. I'd try to go round and apologise.

TH: How are you managing not to argue now?

Dean: When dad was back and we were arguing, it seemed from dad's face he was going to get our heads and smash them together. (The family all smile and laugh.)

TH: So it's really important to have dad back in the family?

Dean: Yeah.

TH: Yeah.

Sometimes you have to hear the bad times, otherwise the family doesn't feel listened to and will also feel discounted. You may lose their engagement. However, as the session progresses the therapist can ask the family to provide her with their positive picture of the client (i.e. the sober person).

Trying to find times when things were OK can be a lot of hard work for the therapist. Returning to the problem is often uppermost on the families mind, but even a small window of positive view can help connect the family to possibilities. Differentiating the person from the drinking behaviour; externalising the problem (White, 1986) enables the problem to be tackled and starts to leave behind blame and identification with the problem behaviour. It is also a reminder to the family of the person behind the addiction. It reawakens competency for them, too.

Finally, what about the therapists? It's all too easy in this field to fall into the trap that many families fall into themselves, that of taking on responsibility for the client. This therapy continually reminds you where responsibility for the behaviour must remain. If the client decides to continue drinking or using, then that has to be their decision. At least if we've seen the family, it would be clear to them also, often by very disparate answers to the miracle question, that their goals were not similar or even likely to converge with the substance user. The partner and family can then make their own decision about what they want to do about that. Their answers to the miracle question can often be an indicator to them about where they might want to go forward in their lives and that their paths may lead in different directions.

Team working

We work as a team, we feel that this is a safe and supportive way to work with families who are beset with difficulties including substance misuse. This gives the client and their family high quality sessions enabling concentrated work to be achieved: every session counts. Single session therapy (Tallman, 1998) should also be included as a possibility. If the work is concentrated and effective it can prove more economical than working on your own. In this multi-disciplinary team, there is a real sharing of skills and responsibility and also a uniform way of working. We still preserve our individuality as therapists, but often our ideas can coincide, so frequently the team behind the screen are about to phone through a question, and the therapist will ask it! Consequently, clients and families, whoever they see in the team, will be getting similar therapy and the same messages about their addiction.

Working as a team means we can assimilate new members, absorb new ideas and try out new strategies. It gives us live supervision and peer supervision. There is a lot of job satisfaction and commitment, our morale is high and burn out rare. Complex family situations can be discussed and taken on by the team. The addicted client may have one team member as an individual counsellor; another member to work with them as a family and, if they move into groupwork, they will encounter other team members as group facilitators. It often gives us a very complete and detailed overview of clients:

The practical benefits of live teams include help in composing letters and reports, confidence in presenting views at case conferences (two people validate, one can be invalidated), effective holiday cover, easy observation of work by trainees, visitors and managers, flexibility for settings without one way screens and to changing to other kinds of work that may be necessary.   (Child and Lieberman, 1995).

Our view of SFBT, as a team, has developed far from our simplistic view of it ten years ago. The work of the key authors referenced in this text have offered us new and exciting ways to build on SFBT basic concepts. We are incorporating it throughout our group programmes and have set up an SFBT group. This runs for three sessions (brief!) and teaches the clients the ideas and concepts of SFBT, so that they can apply it for themselves. Feedback from clients has been overwhelmingly positive. They volunteer that they've felt listened to, and that they feel in control of what's going on. There is an invitation to responsibility and lastly, there is hope.

References

Allen, L. (1996) Combining Solution Focused Ideas with White/Epston Style Therapeutic Letters, *Context*, 26, 34–6.

Berg, I. K., and Miller, S. (1992) *Working with the Problem Drinker. A Solution Focused Approach*, Norton Books. London BT Press.

Berg, I.K., and de Shazer, S. (1993) Making Numbers Talk. Language in Therapy. In Friedman, S. (Ed.) *The New Language of Change*, New York Guildford.

Brisby, T., Baker, S., and Hedderwick, T. (1997) *Under the Influence: Coping with Parents who Drink Too Much*, London, Alcohol Concern.

Burnham, J.B. (1990) *Family Therapy*, Tavistock Library of Social Work Practice.

Child, N., and Lieberman, S. (1995) Lie Teams and Video, *Association of Family Therapy. Information sheet* No. 6b.

Cuijpers, P., Langendoen, Y., and Bijl, R. (1999) Psychiatric Disorders in Adult Children of Problem Drinkers: Prevalence, First Onset and Comparison with Other Risk Factors, *Addiction*, 94 (10), 1489–98.

De Shazer, S. (1985) *Keys to Solutions in Brief Therapy*, New York. W. W. Norton.

De Shazer, S., Berg, I.K., Lipchik, E., Nunnally, E., Molnar, A., Grilgerich, W., and Weiner-Davis, M. (1986) Brief Therapy: Focused Solution Development, *Family Process*, 24, 207–22.

Di Clemente, C., Prochaska, J., Fairhust, S., Velicer, W., Velasophes, M., and Ross, J. (1991) The Process of Smoking Cessation: An Analysis of Pre-contemplation, Contemplation and Preparation Stages of Change, *Journal Consultant Clinical Psychologist*, 9, 295–302.

Dolan, Y. (1991) *Resolving Sexual Abuse*, New York, Newton.

Epston, D., and White, M. (1988–91) *Experience, Contradiction, Narrative and Imagination*, Selected papers, Dulwich Centre Publications.

George, E. (1993) *Solution Focused Brief Therapy*, London: BT Press.

George, E., Iveson, C., and Ratner, H. (1990) *Problem to Solution Brief Therapy with Individuals and Families*, London, BT Press.

Substance Misuse and Child Care

George, E., Iveson, C., and Ratner, H. (1990) *Problem to Solution*, London, BT Press.

Housten, A., Kork, S., and Macleod, M. (1997) *Beyond the Limit: Children who Live with Parental Alcohol Misuse*, London, Childline.

Laybourn, A., Brown, J., and Hill, M. (1996) *Hurting on the Inside Children's Experiences of Parental Alcohol Misuse*, Avebury.

Long, A., and Mullen, B. (1994) An Exploration of Women's Perceptions of the Major Factors that Contributed to their Alcohol Abuse, *Journal of Advanced Nursing*, 19, 623–39.

McGoldrick, M: and Gerson, R. (1985) *Genograms in Family Assessments*, Norton and Co.

Miller, W. R., and Rollnick, S. (1991) *Motivational Interviewing: Preparing People to Change Addictive Behaviour*, New York, Guilford.

O'Hanlon, W. (1987) *Taproots: Underlying Principles of Milton Erickson's Therapy and Hypnosis*, New York, Norton.

Schoor, E., and Beach, R. (1993) Pseudo-independence in Adolescent Drug Abuse: A Family Systems Perspective Family Therapy, *Journal of Family Therapy*, 20, 3.

Spak, L., Spak, F., and Allebeck, P. (1997) Factors in Childhood and Youth Predicting Alcohol Dependence and Abuse in Swedish Women: Findings from a General Population Study, *Alcohol and Alcoholism*, 32, 3, 267–74.

Stafford, D. (1992) *Children of Alcoholics*, London, Piatkus.

Swett, C., and Halpert, M. (1994) High Rates of Alcohol Problems and History of Physical and Sexual Abuse Among Women Inpatients, *American Journal of Drug and Alcohol Abuse*, 20(2), 263–72.

Tallman, M. (1998) *Single Session Therapy*, London, BT Press.

Velleman, R. (1993) *Alcohol and the Family*, Institute of Alcohol Studies.

Velleman, R. (1995) Conference Address, 21.11.95. Leicestershire Alcohol Advice Centre.

White, M. (1986) Negative Explanation, Restraint and Double Description: A Template for Family Therapy, *Family Process*, 25, 169–84.

Woodside, M; (1988) Research on Children of Alcoholics; Past and Future, *British Journal of Addiction*, 83, 785–92.

Zeitlin, W. (1994) Children with Alcohol Misusing Parents, *British Medical Bulletin*, 50, 1, 139–51.

10 Establishing and Developing Co-operative Links Between Substance Misuse and Child Protection Systems

Michael Murphy and Gary Oulds

Introduction

This chapter is about inter-agency collaboration; it is about staff from different agencies working together. In the fields of child protection and substance misuse, staff have endeavoured, for many years, to promote co-operative working within their own systems. Thus, during the 25-five years that followed the death of Maria Colwell in 1973, child protection staff have been exhorted to develop and maintain their inter-agency collaboration to prevent further child deaths (DHSS, 1974; DHSS, 1988; DoH, 1991 and DoH, 1999).

This chapter is different in that it concerns the establishment and development of these co-operative links not just between agencies, but also between systems, two distinct and determinedly separate systems. So, rather than just working across agency boundaries, it is about staff working across the boundaries between systems: *inter-system* as well as *inter-agency* working.

Whilst planning a national conference (Bolton ACPC, 19th February 1999) that concerned the crossover between substance misuse and child protection, we realised that participants were coming from two substantially different backgrounds. They would not only be arriving from different agencies but also from different systems and cultures:

> *Working together, however, is complex because of the different legislation and guidance concerning illicit drug use, and the care of children and the different perspectives of the agencies who are concerned with both.*
> (SCODA, 1997, p16).

To make the conference a success, we had to help both 'sides' participate and gain equally from the experience. We were inviting two different sets of people to work and learn together and we would have to create the right conditions to ensure that they were enabled to do so.

But what were the implications of this presumption for practice in the field? If we were obliged to make a special effort to allow both sides to come together at the conference, what special effort needed to be made, in practice, to help staff communicate and collaborate together? If that special effort were not made, what would be the effect on their work? These questions constitute the underpinning challenge of this chapter which is split into three main sections:

The first, entitled *Why bother?* examines the essential questions (a) why should the two systems be concerned about co-operative working? What is the motivating force behind this working together? And (b) what would happen if they did not work together?

The second section, *Barriers to collaboration* explores the difficulties that stand in the way of inter-system working. Why, if co-operative working is so essential, is it so difficult to achieve in practice?

The third section *Promoting inter-system collaboration* seeks to help managers and practitioners promote co-operative working and offers some practical solutions to the problems of the inter-system collaboration.

Why bother?

Substance misuse and child abuse have been defined and redefined as social problems over many years:

> *The emergence of a social problem is contingent on the organisation of group activities with reference to defining some putative condition as a problem and asserting the need for eradication, ameliorating or otherwise changing that condition.*   (Kitsuse and Spector, 1973, p415).

Serious concern about child abuse has been present in British society for over 125 years (Behlmer, 1982) with consequent legislation and social action that attempted to address this problem. The modern British child protection system can be said to have begun in 1974 with the government's response to the Maria Colwell inquiry (Corby, 1993; Murphy, 1995 and Parton, 1985). The system that was established in 1974 has undergone several changes since that time, but its basic structure remains the same (see Appendix 2).

Societal concern about the misuse of substances (mainly but not exclusively alcohol) had begun even earlier in our society and the connection, in the Victorian era, between substance and child misuse had been well established (Behlmer, 1982 and Gordon, 1989). The modern concern about substance (non-alcohol) misuse and the system set up to deal with it, can usefully be linked to the significant increase in opiate misuse in the 1980s and the associated concern with the spread of the HIV virus.

So societal concern and social construction of both problems has been present for a considerable time and the subsequent systems set up to deal with these problems are now well established. However, the concern of the late Victorian and Edwardian eras that closely linked substance misuse to family violence, has not been transferred into the modern era. For example, in the Maria Colwell inquiry (DHSS, 1974) Mr Kepple's (Maria's stepfather) substance misuse was largely ignored by the staff concerned and by the inquiry. So the two modern systems have developed independently of each other, following their own paths without much regard for the direction or purpose of the other.

These systems may well have continued this unconnected development were it not for a growing recognition, promoted by research from the USA (Murphy et al., 1991; Jaudes, Eckwo and Voorhis, 1995 and Dore, Doris and Wright, 1995) that they seemed to have clients, concerns and difficulties very much in common. This research indicated that not only did they share many clients but that substance misuse and child abuse impacted significantly on each other:

> *. . . in cases of serious substance abuse, unless this problem is identified and treated, there is very little point in beginning other forms of treatment. Continuing substance abuse has a high probability of undoing other interventions.* (Murphy et al., 1991, p209).

Still further, seemingly unrelated developments in one system could have a dramatic impact on the other. Dore et al. (1995) describe the significant increase in child protection caseloads (in the USA) due largely to the increasing use of crack cocaine:

> *. . . the most important factor in skyrocketing protective services caseloads is an increase in parental substance abuse, particularly the crack form of cocaine.* (p532).

So the motivating factors behind the establishment of co-operative links seem to be that:

- As both systems hold a substantial number of clients in common, some level of liaison would be useful.
- As progress in child care or substance misuse treatment will be limited by a crisis in the other arena, all practitioners have an investment in making sure that work in the other system goes well.
- From a strategic point of view, significant changes in the substance arena may critically impact on the child protection system.

Although the above research was conducted in the USA, in the late 1980s and early 1990s it has become increasingly clear that this message was also true for Britain. In 1989 the Standing Conference on Drug Abuse (SCODA) published the first guidance in this area, warning about the possible negative effects of substance misuse on family interaction. SCODA's later guidance (1997) emphasised:

> *The effective safeguarding of children and provision of support for families requires all professionals and agencies to work together on both strategic and operational levels.* (SCODA, 1997, p5).

In the 1990s, government guidance on child protection has included warnings to practitioners about substance misuse:

> *A parent's practical caring skills may be diminished by misuse of drugs and/or alcohol. Some substance misuse may give rise to mental states or behaviour which put children at risk of injury, psychological distress, or neglect.* (DoH, 1999, p22).

Within our own working area, since 1992, we have discovered that the number of known drug users has increased by 300 per cent. More concerning, 46 per cent of these users have dependent children. Substance misuse is a major issue in referrals to our advice and assessment (social work) teams and our fostering and adoption panel. Most disturbing of all, and in this we mirror the experience in the USA (Murphy et al., 1991) of those children on our child protection register over 30 per cent come from families where substance misuse is present and over 75 per cent of all child care court proceedings involve some level of substance misuse. For us therefore, this concern about the crossover between the two issues was not some 'rumour from abroad', but a current reality for our staff and the systems for which they work.

What would happen if the two systems did not establish co-operative links? At first glance this simple question begs an equally simple response, but this issue is more complex than it first appears. At the Bolton conference it became apparent that the quantity and quality of co-operative working and co-ordination varied immensely between one area and another, and that it was normal for levels of co-operation to fluctuate even within a given area. In Bermondsey, Forrester discerned that:

> *In the 34 most recent case conferences involving substance-abusing parents, only four specialist substance abuse workers were invited ... only two of those attended.* (Forrester, 2000, p242).

Practice scenario 1: Helen was the manager of a substance team in the Bigtown area. She noted that the relationships between her own team and several child care teams was excellent, with regular, friendly contact and collaboration. However, with one particular child care team the contact was infrequent and begrudging. Helen made sure that she was a regular visitor to the team, cultivated a friendly relationship with the team leader and slowly the atmosphere of hostility began to change. She also encouraged her staff to get involved in mutual 'shadowing' arrangements with that particular team.

Participants within the conference workshop admitted that even when the quantity and quality of collaboration were low, they still were obliged to have some communication with practitioners from the other arena. But in some locations this contact was ad-hoc, begrudging and very unsatisfactory.

Figure 1. Typology of co-ordination (Developed from Hallett, 1992)

Level four *central policy co-ordination* policy development and central government level

Level three *programme co-ordination* policy and procedure development at an ACPC/DAT/agency level

Level two *systematic co-ordination* planning meetings, CP conferences, core groups etc.

Level one *ad hoc co-ordination* conversations/letters/phone calls between front-line staff

It seems that in the worst scenario, some systems become stuck in level one of Hallett's (1992) typology of co-ordination (Figure 1). In these systems ad-hoc communication between front-line staff was perceived to be unsatisfactory and not allied to the more formal co-ordination at levels two and three.

It seems impossible, therefore, for the two systems to maintain complete separation and non co-operation. Some systems do become stuck in a series of unsatisfactory communications between front line staff and never go on to develop the more systematic forms of collaboration that assist staff in communicating, planning and working together. If this is the case, this form of communication will usually be experienced as being unsatisfactory. It is only when more established and formal communication is achieved that those further levels of collaboration are possible. Within Bolton we have developed a pyramid that expresses a different way of portraying these different levels of collaboration (see Figure 2) beginning with complete separation and ending with more highly developed forms of collaboration.

Figure 2. Pyramid of co-operation (Murphy and Oulds, 1999)

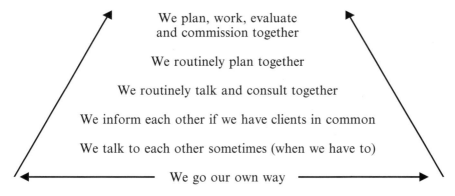

We plan, work, evaluate and commission together

We routinely plan together

We routinely talk and consult together

We inform each other if we have clients in common

We talk to each other sometimes (when we have to)

We go our own way

Barriers to collaboration

Why is this collaboration between practitioners, agencies and systems so difficult to achieve? What are the barriers to collaboration that staff must overcome? Scott (1997) has argued that the blocks to co-operative working must be understood from both the individual/professional level and from the organisational/agency level.

On an individual level, it is sometimes difficult to act in a collaborative way even with members of our own agency and practitioner group. When we are asked to collaborate with practitioners outside our sphere, many extra barriers are encountered:

> *... practitioners are brought up or accultured in one agency. The practitioner in a particular agency will speak that particular practice language, will understand the roles and structure within that practice system and will automatically and unconsciously see the world through that single agency perspective.*   (Murphy, 2000).

Practitioners see the world from their different perspectives, they hold different professional values and consequently they behave in different ways:

> *... Professionals tend to focus on the needs of their specific client group. When the needs of their client are at odds with the needs of others in the family they may feel the need to advocate on their behalf. This may result in polarised views which block effective joint working.*
>
> (Cleaver et al., 1999, p100).

These barriers to collaboration are enhanced by differences in language, roles, priorities, training, power and traditional ways of working (Murphy, 1995). Furthermore we all harbour a deep ignorance of how other practitioners think: we see practice behaviour and ascribe (often wrongly) all kinds of meaning to it. Because of this, on an individual level, communication and subsequent collaboration are difficult to achieve.

Practice scenario 2: Kiren, a practitioner in a child care team, was experiencing severe difficulty in communicating with staff from a local substance team. On a joint training course she was encouraged to explore how members of that team worked and why they behaved as they did. Kiren expressed her amazement that she had survived so long without understanding some of the basic underpinnings of the other team's work and philosophy. She left the course with a wholly different understanding of how the substance team thought and worked.

These 'normal' practice impediments that affect individual practitioners are exaggerated by the barriers that exist between systems. On an agency, system or organisational basis, this difference in perspective, role and behaviour can be magnified by differences in legislation, policies and philosophy. These create organisational barriers to co-operation:

Figure 3.

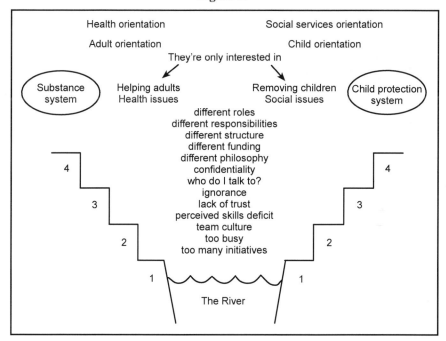

. . . agencies who work with children and those who work with adults often have different philosophies and policies. Child-centred agencies may not understand or feel confident in dealing with drug users, whilst specialist drug services may not understand the needs of children or child protection procedures. (SCODA, 1997, p4).

Even if individual practitioners see the necessity for greater collaboration, if the organisational impediments to collaboration have not been addressed, such collaboration can be difficult to achieve.

Practice scenario 3: At a review of a case of child mistreatment, it became clear that a particular substance agency had not appropriately reported their concerns about the injured child. Closer inspection revealed that there had been confusion around the issue of child abuse and confidentiality, but more seriously the substance agency had not been aware of the ACPC's procedures or protocols and therefore remained in ignorance of appropriate protective responses.

The image that we have used to portray these barriers to collaboration is of a valley, with the two systems on either side and in the middle a swift flowing river full of the impediments to inter-professional, inter-agency and inter-system collaboration (Figure 3). The task of practitioners, managers and central government departments, is to bridge the river to overcome impediments and to achieve collaborative working.

The next section examines how we might build a bridge across this river to enhance the quantity and quality of our inter-system collaboration.

Promoting inter-system collaboration

Successful inter-organisational activity is no arid, managerial exercise. The challenge is to create the right climate for collaboration, to recognise the different contributions that participants can make, and to devise organisational arrangements and incentive structures that foster collaborative working. (Hudson, 2000, p254).

The promotion of inter-system collaboration is an evolutionary process that involves long-term, rather than short term, change. It is preferable for collaborative initiatives to have a positive motivation rather than be a sequel of a negative incident (for example a child death) because such incidents often promote mutual incrimination and distrust.

During the conference, we asked workshop participants to check out the health of collaborative links in their area by discussing the nine listed questions (see Figure 4).

In the subsequent discussion it became clear that no two areas enjoy the same levels of co-operation or employ the same methods of promoting

Figure 4. Co-operative links in your area (nine checks)

1. How often do members of either system consult with staff from the other?
2. Do substance misuse staff ever 'trigger' child protection enquiries/ procedures?
3. Do you have joint policy protocols for the management of childcare/substance problems?
4. Do you run (interagency) courses on (a) awareness raising about child protection or substance issues and (b) the crossover between substance misuse and child protection?
5. How often are members of the substance misuse system involved in (a) CP conferences (b) CP core groups and (c) joint assessment work?
6. Do your substance staff routinely assess parenting skills/ability?
7. Do your ACPC, DAT, social services dept and substance system have established channels of communication/co-operation?
8. Do you gather data or organise research on the crossover between substance misuse and child care issues?
9. Have you established any special posts which 'bridge' the divide between the two systems?

inter-system collaboration. The ideas that participants suggested to promote collaboration could usefully be divided into four:

- organisational developments
- professional/practice developments
- joint project developments
- training developments

Organisational developments

For collaboration to become the norm within an area, the key agencies and groups of agencies must provide the organisational framework for that collaboration to take place and to be sustained:

> *All areas should have written policies and guidelines . . . Local authorities and agencies should disseminate their policies widely . . . Health and local authorities should have a shared strategy for developing services that provides the basis for joint commissioning of services.* (SCODA, 1997, p6)

If policies and procedures are not present then staff will find sustained collaboration more difficult to achieve. It is also important that these policies and procedures are reviewed on a regular basis to check if they are still relevant, still up-to-date, still being followed and still useful to practitioners. Levin et al. (2000) in a recent NISW survey discovered that half of their sample had established protocols for inter-agency work in this area (often based on the SCODA guidelines).

Finally, because each system is affected by different initiatives, guidance and legislation, when working out the response to a new initiative or guidance it is essential to consider its consequent (often unintended) effect on the other system as well. Although the government may aim to champion 'joined up' thinking, the initiatives of different government departments can leave systems struggling to maintain their 'joined up' working:

> *The barriers between the various services extend to a knowledge of individual service innovations, which may be regarded as marginal within their own field and hard to publicise to other service areas.*
> (Levin et al., 2000, p24).

Professional practice developments

It is important that practitioners and managers have positive contact with staff from the other system. If it is not possible to achieve this through joint training events, this contact can be achieved through mutual 'shadowing', attending team meetings or inter-team briefings (see Practice Scenario 1).

In some areas, one successful method of promoting contact has been to establish a special interest group for practitioners from both systems, where staff can discuss difficult mutual issues away from the demands of day-to-day casework. Levin (et al., 2000) have reported that:

Some agencies had time-tabled regular cross-division and cross-agency sessions to consider interface issues. They report that this has made the work more visible and has allowed them to move on from case-by-case discussion to strategic approaches to the work.   (p25).

Joint project developments
One very effective way of developing collaboration is to create posts or projects that seek to bridge the gap between the two systems. This might include:

• Developing a research project with members from both services to investigate the level of crossover between the two systems or to research the effects of substance misuse on families and children.
• Establishing a practice project, perhaps a centre for intensive work with a small number of families and children, with staff from both systems.
• Joint sponsoring of specific, specialist posts: for example the employment of a specialist midwife for work with mothers who misuse substances whose children may be involved in the child protection system.
• Establishing a collaborative campaign (e.g. keep methadone away from children campaign) that positively draws staff in from both systems to achieve a common goal.

Training developments

Inter-agency trainingcan be a highly effective way of promoting a common and shared understanding of the respective roles and responsibilities of different professionals and can contribute to effective working relationships.   (DoH, 1999, p97).

Appropriate training can be very effective in promoting inter-system understanding and collaboration. Training works on two levels: the first is to inform participants about the 'world' of the other system and the second is to explore the areas of crossover between the two systems:

Professionals who work primarily with children may need training to recognise and identify parents problems and the effects these may have on children. Equally, training for professionals working with adults should cover the impact parental problems may have on children. Joint training between adults and children staff can be useful.   (DoH, 1999, p11).

It is important to involve staff from both systems as participants and facilitators in this training to ensure that the training does not become too lopsided by over concentration on the side of one system at the expense of the other.

Conclusion
This chapter has been concerned with the development of inter-system collaboration. In the 1970s and early 1980s the modern substance and child

protection systems have progressed separately without regard to the others developmental pathways. In the late 1980s and 1990s it has become clear that the two systems have much in common, not least that they share individual clients, families and mutually impacting concerns. This chapter has discussed the reality of the crossover between the two systems and examined what might be the result of their continued separation. Separate development, as we have seen, is not a practical or productive option for either system, it is wasteful of energy and resources and is not in the interest of children or parents.

However, having established that there seems no alternative to developing inter-system collaboration, it is unwise to underestimate the magnitude of the blocks to that collaboration. The chapter has examined the professional and organisational impediments to developing collaboration. We have concluded by examining the different ways of promoting collaboration between the two systems using organisational, professional, developmental and training initiatives and interventions.

Developing inter-system collaboration in this area is about changing narrow, single system ways of thinking. It is about using that new way of thinking to instigate changes in collaboration at all levels of involvement, from basic grade practitioner to government department. This change is more likely to be evolutionary rather than revolutionary, involving changes in mindset as well as changes within systems.

References

Ammerman, T., Kolko, D., Kirisci, L., Blackson, T., and Dawes, M. (1999) Child Abuse Potential in Parents with Histories of Substance Use Disorder, *Child Abuse and Neglect* 23, 12, 1225–38.

Behlmer, G. (1982) *Child Abuse and Moral Reform in England 1870–1908*, Stanford, University Press.

Cleaver, H., Urell, I. and Aldgate, J. (1999) *Children's Needs: Parenting Capacity*, London, HMSO.

Corby, B. (1993) *Child Abuse: Towards a Knowledge Base*, Buckingham, OU Press.

DHSS (1974) *Report of The Committee of Inquiry into the Care and Supervision Provided in Relation to Maria Colwell*, London, HMSO.

DHSS (1988) *Working Together: A Guide to Inter-agency Co-operation for the Protection of Children from Abuse*, London, HMSO.

DoH (1991) *Working Together under the 1989 Children Act*, London, HMSO.

DoH (1999) *Working Together to Safeguard Children: A Guide to Inter-agency Working to Safeguard and Promote the Welfare of Children*, London, HMSO.

Dore, M., Doris, J., and Wright, P. (1995) Identifying Substance Abuse in Maltreating Families: A Child Welfare Challenge. *Child Abuse and Neglect*, 19, 5, 531–44.

Forresster, D. (2000) Parental Substance Abuse and Child Protection in a British Sample, *Child Abuse Review*, 9, 235–46

Gordon, L. (1989) *Heroes of their own Lives: The Politics and History of Family Violence, Boston 1880–1960*, London, Virago.

Hallett, C., and Birchall, E. (1992) *Inter-agency Co-ordination in Child Protection*, London, HMSO.

Hudson, B. (2000) *Inter-agency Collaboration: A Sceptical View*. in Brechin, A., Brown, H., and Eby, M. (Eds) *Critical Practice in Health and Social Care*, London, OU/Sage.

Jaudes, P., Ekwo, E., and Voorhis, J. (1995) Association of Drug Abuse and Child Abuse, *Child Abuse and Neglect*, 19. 9, 1065–76.

Kitsuse, J., and Spector, M. (1973) Towards a Sociology of Social Problems, *Journal of Social Problems*, 408–19.

Levin, E., Kearney, P., and Rosen, G. (2000) Fitting it Together, *Community Care*, 3rd–9th August, 24–5.

Murphy, J.M., Jellinek, M., Quinn, D., Smith, G., Poitrast, F., and Goshko, M. (1991) Substance Abuse and Serious Child Mistreatment: Prevalence, Risk and Outcome in a Court Sample, *Child Abuse and Neglect*, 15, 3, 197–211.

Murphy, M. (1995) *Working together in Child Protection: An Exploration of the Multi-disciplinary Task and System*, Aldershot, Arena.

Murphy, M. (2000) *The Inter-agency Trainer* in Charles, M., and Hendry, E. (Eds) *Training Together to Safeguard Children*, London, NSPCC/PIAT.

Parton, N. (1985) *The Politics of Child Abuse*, Basingstoke, Macmillan.

SCODA (1997) *Drug Using Parents: Policy Guidelines for Inter-agency Working*, London, LGA Publications.

Scott, D. (1997) Inter-agency Conflict: An Ethnographic Study, *Child and Family Social Work*, 12, 2, 73–80.

Appendix 1 Facts about Drugs

This appendix is drawn from the ISDD *Drug Abuse Briefing*. It offers information on amphetamine, cocaine and crack cocaine, heroin and other opiates.

Amphetamines

Amphetamines are synthetic stimulants similar in structure to norepiniphrine, a naturally occurring chemical in the brain. There are three types of amphetamine, the strongest being methylamphetamine, followed by dexamphetamine, and then laevo or d'l-amphetamine. Amphetamines are legitimately sold as powders or tablets under names such as Dexedrine (dexamphetamine sulphate) and Ritalin (methylphenidate hydrochloride).

Amphetamine sulphate or speed, the name given to illicitly produced amphetamine, is usually a mixture of d'l-amphetamine and dexamphetamine, cut to a retail strength of around 10–12 per cent. Adulterants include caffeine, glucose powder and sometimes chalk.

Recent newcomers on the amphetamine scene are two potent versions of the drug. Amphetamine base, which usually comes as a paste, is a form the drug takes during manufacture previous to being crystallised into a powder. Smoked or swallowed base can be 50 per cent or more pure amphetamine. An import from the USA, methylamphetamine in crystalline form, known as Ice, is a smokeable or injectable form of amphetamine powder, similar in its relation to speed as crack is to cocaine.

Legal status

All the amphetamines and similar stimulants are prescription only drugs under the Medicines Act and are also controlled under the Misuse of Drugs Act. Doctors can still prescribe them and patients possess them if they have been prescribed, but otherwise their unauthorised production, supply or possession is an offence. It is also an offence to allow premises to be used for producing or supplying these drugs. Amphetamine and its analogues are Class B drugs, but if these are prepared for injection, the increased penalties of Class A apply.

Prevalence

Recreational use of amphetamines by teenagers (such as 'mods' taking 'purple hearts') in the early and mid sixties died out, as the pills became less available. However, amphetamine use has never gone away. Use of amphetamine powder was common among certain youth subcultures throughout the 1970s and 1980s and on the back of dance culture, use has increased substantially through the 1990s. Currently around 9 per cent of the adult population (16–59) have used the drug. However, as with other drugs, the level of use is higher for younger people. Around 21 per cent of those aged 19 to 24 years, said they have used amphetamines at least once, with around half of these respondents having used in the last year. Amphetamine injectors tend to be older than other amphetamine users, and have usually been using the drug for a long period of time. Use of amphetamine base is reported to be on the increase, particularly on the dance scene and amongst those choosing to inject, primarily due to its alleged purity and greater strength.

Licit and illicit use

In the 1950s and 1960s they were widely prescribed to treat depression and to suppress appetite, but are now recommended only for the treatment of extreme over-activity (hyperkinesia) in children, for which Ritalin is prescribed, and a pathological tendency to fall asleep (narcolepsy).

Amphetamines may be smoked, dabbed (orally consumed by dabbing small amounts each time onto the finger and into the mouth) or dissolved in soft drinks and drunk, but the illicitly manufactured powders available today are generally sniffed up the nose or injected. In some groups the drug is used as required to aid performance at manual or intellectual tasks, in others for purely recreational purposes. The drug's quality as an appetite suppressant also makes the drug popular as a slimming aid.

An occasional user might take a few weeks to consume ½gm, while a heavy user who has developed substantial tolerance to the drug's effects, might consume anything up to several grams a day of relatively low purity substance. The smokeable form Ice is usually smoked in glass pipes similar to those used by crack users. Intravenous amphetamine use has been part of the UK drug scene since the late 1960s.

Price

The powder retails at about £10–15/gm but can be much cheaper. A typical £5 'wrap' of 400–500mg of powder contains 50mg of amphetamine. Amphetamine base sells for roughly £10–£25/gm, Ice, or crystal 'rock' for roughly £25/gm.

Short term use

Amphetamines arouse and activate the user much as the body's natural adrenaline does in the face of emergencies or stress. Breathing and heart rate speed up, the pupils widen, and appetite lessens. The user feels more alert, energetic, confident and cheerful and less bored or tired. With higher doses, intense exhilaration, rapid flow of ideas and feelings of greatly increased physical and mental capacity are common.

With some people however (especially as the body's energy stores become depleted) the predominant feelings may be anxiety, irritability, and restlessness. High doses, especially if frequently repeated over a few days, can produce delirium, panic, hallucinations and feelings of persecution ('amphetamine psychosis') which gradually disappear as the drug is eliminated from the body. The effects of a single dose last about three to four hours, and leave the user feeling tired: it can take a couple of days for the body to fully recover, even after small doses.

Long-term use

The mood-elevating effects of synthetic stimulants can lead to psychological dependence. After a 'run' of stimulant use or after long-term regular use, the user is likely to feel deeply depressed, lethargic and hungry, because amphetamines merely postpone fatigue and hunger, but they do not satisfy the needs of the body and mind for rest and nourishment. However, abrupt cessation of stimulant use generally requires no medical assistance as physiological processes are not severely disrupted. Tolerance develops to the stimulant effects of the amphetamines, so frequent users are tempted to increase the dose. At this stage toxic effects are liable to develop, including delusions, hallucinations and feelings of paranoia. Many experienced users are aware that their paranoia is drug induced, but sometimes these feelings lead to hostility as stimulant users defend themselves against imagined attacks. These symptoms can persist for a time after drug taking has stopped, but will eventually abate. In a few people they develop into a psychotic state, from which it can take several months to fully recover.

Heavy, prolonged stimulant use debilitates the user due to lack of sleep and food, and lowers resistance to disease. Users who inject the drug also run the same risks to health as those injecting any other drug.

Cocaine and crack

Cocaine (cocaine hydrochloride) is a white powder derived from the leaves of the Andean coca shrub, erythroxylum coca, with powerful stimulant properties similar to those of amphetamines.

Due to its expense, cocaine has come to be seen as a 'jet set' drug, the illicit equivalent of champagne, and in some South American producer countries cocaine profits are a major corrupting influence on the economy.

Cocaine is injected, sometimes mixed with heroin, but more commonly a small amount is sniffed up the nose through a tube and absorbed into the blood supply via the nasal membranes. Cocaine is also smoked through a process known as freebasing whereby the cocaine base is 'freed' from the acid hydrochloride. 'Crack' is simply freebased cocaine produced by an easier method resulting in small rocks of cocaine each about the size of a raisin.

Legal status

Cocaine, its various salts, and the leaves of the coca plant, are now controlled in Class A of the Misuse of Drugs Act. The only restriction on cocaine prescribing for therapeutic purposes, is that, as with some opiates, a doctor must be licensed by the Home Office before they can use the drug to treat anything other than physical illness. This means that most doctors cannot prescribe cocaine as a way of dealing with addiction. Such use is, however, very uncommon. It is also illegal to allow premises to be used for producing or supplying cocaine.

Prevalence
In general, the expense of cocaine can still be expected to limit its regular use to a small percentage of the population. Cocaine has been used by 3 per cent of the adult population, around 6 per cent for those aged 20–24. There are some indications that cocaine use is increasing among those who attend clubs, particularly in the South East, where supply appears to be rising and prices dropping.

Licit and illicit use
In the mid 1970s cocaine sniffing gained popularity especially where there was style (fast), champagne (bubbly) and money (lots). This was originally located in the world of entertainment, especially the music and film industries and then in the 1980s became anecdotally a 'fashion accessory' for the younger members of the City of London's Square Mile. It also came to be used on an occasional basis by a broader section of the drug using population.

During the 1990s, a smokeable variety known as crack has become common in areas of traditional chronic problematic drug use, mainly (but not exclusively) inner-city areas suffering acute social deprivation.

The typical 'weekend' user might sniff ¼gm or so over the weekend; regular users with sufficient resources might consume 1–2gms a day. In some areas cocaine powder has become more difficult to obtain owing to the amount of powder being converted to crack. Because the effects wear off very quickly, users can get through several grams (and thus hundreds of pounds) at a stretch.

Price
Although more expensive than amphetamine, people already involved in drug taking circles can currently obtain cocaine at around £40–£80/gm averaged out for the whole of the United Kingdom. The purer the cocaine the higher the price, but prices above £100 are uncommon. Prices seem to be lower in the South East where £50 can typically buy the user a gram of 40–50 per cent pure cocaine. Crack is available in many parts of the country retailing at around £25 weighing 150mg and around 88 per cent pure, although samples of 100 per cent purity are not unknown. Smaller slivers of crack may be sliced from a 'rock' and sold more cheaply.

Short term use
Like amphetamine, cocaine produces physiological arousal accompanied by exhilaration, feelings of well-being, decreased hunger, indifference to pain

and fatigue, and feelings of great physical strength and mental capacity. Sometimes these desired effects are replaced by anxiety or panic. When sniffed, the psychological effects peak after about 15–30 minutes and then diminish, meaning the dose may have to be repeated every 20 minutes to maintain the effect. When smoked as crack the effects are almost immediate and very intense but more short-lived.

Large doses or a 'spree' of quickly repeated doses over a period of hours can lead to an extreme state of agitation, anxiety, paranoia, and perhaps hallucination. As with the amphetamine psychosis, these effects generally resolve themselves as the drug is eliminated from the body. The after-effects of cocaine use include fatigue and depression, but are less noticeable than the corresponding effects after amphetamine use. These effects are said to be stronger for crack use. Excessive doses can cause death from respiratory or heart failure, but these are rare. As with heroin, cocaine is likely to be adulterated with substances which may be harmful when injected.

Long-term use

Neither tolerance nor heroin-like withdrawal symptoms occur with repeated use of cocaine, but users may well develop a strong psychological dependence on the grandiose feelings of physical and mental well-being afforded by the drug, and are often tempted to step up the dose. After discontinuing, the user will feel fatigued, sleepy and depressed (though not as severely as following repeated amphetamine use), all of which reinforce the temptation to repeat the dose. Dependence appears more likely and more severe and its onset more rapid if cocaine is smoked.

With chronic frequent use, increasingly unpleasant symptoms develop which generally persuade people to 'give it a break'. Euphoria is replaced by an uncomfortable state of restlessness, hyperexcitability, nausea, insomnia and weight loss. With continued use this may develop into a state of mind similar to paranoid psychosis. Regular users who do not use sufficiently to become manifestly psychotic may nevertheless appear chronically nervous, excitable and paranoid, and confused exhaustion due to lack of sleep is not unusual. All these effects generally clear up once use is discontinued. Repeated sniffing damages the membranes lining the nose and may also damage the structure separating the nostrils. Repeated smoking may cause respiratory problems such as cracked, wheezy breathing and also partial loss of voice. Long-term injection produces abscesses and injecting generally exposes the user to the special risks of this method of administration.

Heroin, methadone and other opiates

Opiates are a group of drugs derived from the opium poppy, with generally similar effects, notably analgesia. Opiates and their synthetic equivalents are sometimes collectively known as 'opioids' although strictly speaking, the term 'opioids' only applies to the synthetic drugs of this type. As well as being prescribed as painkillers, opiates have medical uses as cough suppressants and anti-diarrhoea agents.

The relative speed of action of heroin and the relative absence of undesirable side-effects associated with other opiates (e.g. nausea, vomiting, constipation) have made it the opiate preferred by many drug users, while its potency relative to other opiates makes smuggling of smaller amounts more profitable. As with other drugs intravenous injection maximises the effects.

Legal status

Opiates are controlled under the Misuse of Drugs Act, making it illegal to supply or to possess them without a prescription, and penalising unauthorised production, import or export. It is also an offence to allow premises to be used for producing or supplying these drugs.

Only specially licensed doctors can prescribe heroin, dipipanone (and cocaine) for anything other than physical illness. This means most doctors cannot prescribe these drugs as a way of dealing with dependence. Apart from this, all opiates can be prescribed for their normal therapeutic uses. Heroin, morphine, opium, methadone, dipipanone and pethidine appear in Class A of the Act.

Prevalence

Since the late 1970s, opiate availability, use and dependence have all substantially increased, largely due to the increased availability of illicitly imported heroin. Until 1997, doctors were obliged to notify the Home Office of any opiate (and cocaine) addicts they attended. During 1996, around 40,000 were notified to the Home Office; this may underestimate the total opiate using population of the UK by anything from a factor of 3–5. Over half the opiate addicts first notified in 1996 were aged under 25.

Licit and illicit use

Opiate powders can be swallowed or dissolved in water and injected. Heroin is rarely swallowed (as this is relatively ineffective) but can be sniffed like cocaine or smoked. When smoked, heroin powder is heated on tin foil and the fumes inhaled, commonly through a small tube, a practice known as 'chasing the dragon'.

Opium itself is either eaten or smoked. Some opiate mixtures are effectively rendered non-injectable by the substances used to dissolve the powder, one reason why methadone mixture is frequently prescribed to opiate addicts. Chronic users generally inject, but recreational use of heroin has developed among people in their late teens, the drug being sniffed, smoked and injected. In an era of greater awareness about the dangers of injecting, statistics indicate that the numbers of those injecting heroin is falling slightly. Besides those dependent on heroin, some people are dependent on synthetic opiates obtained by theft from pharmacies or from doctors. In times of difficulty it is not unusual for opiate users to resort to tranquillisers or sedatives, or to drinking large quantities of opiate based cough medicines available without prescription from pharmacies; some people restrict their opiate misuse to these preparations.

Price

Illicit heroin averaging 30–50 per cent pure retails at around £50 to £80/gm, depending on where in the country it is sold. Smaller quantities such as ¼gm bags retail at around £20 to £25. An addict might use ¼gm each day. More and cheaper heroin, coupled with the fact that heroin users and dealers no longer form an insular network, mean that the drug is presently fairly easy to obtain. At street level it is likely to have been diluted (or adulterated) with a variety of powders of similar appearance, such as glucose powder, chalk dust, caffeine, quinine, flour and talcum powder and other drug substances like phenobarbitone powder. Recent evidence shows that purity levels have been falling from roughly 50 per cent in 1995 to 35 per cent in 1998. Methadone retails for a price of £1 per 10mls. A user will typically buy in quantities of 50ml to 100ml, or in ampules of 25ml at £25 per unit.

Short term use

Pure opiates in moderate doses produce a range of generally mild physical effects, apart from analgesia, and a number of these have medical applications. Like sedatives they depress nervous system activity, including reflex functions such as coughing, respiration and heart rate. They also dilate blood vessels (giving a feeling of warmth) and depress bowel activity, resulting in constipation. Even at levels sufficient to produce euphoria, there is little interference with sensation, motor skills or intellect. At higher doses, sedation takes over and the user becomes drowsy and contented. Excessive doses produce stupor and coma. Death from respiratory failure is possible, but unlikely unless there are contributory factors, such as other depressant drugs used at the same time, loss of tolerance, or unexpected potency. There can also be fatal reactions to injected adulterants. With the uncertain composition and purity of street heroin, adverse reactions are an ever-present possibility. With more people coming forward for treatment, there are increasing numbers of people who are overdosing on prescribed methadone.

There is much confusion about the initial heroin experience. A large proportion of people report drowsiness, warmth, well-being, and content-ment. Pleasurable feelings are associated with the fact that opiates induce relaxed detachment from the impact of pain and anxiety, and from desires for food and sex, even at the same time as the person remains fully aware. Along with or instead of these reactions, first use (especially injection) is often accompanied by nausea and vomiting. Whether this deters people will depend on their motivations for continuing and the strength of the euphoria. These unpleasant reactions quickly disappear with repeated doses. Injection into the veins intensifies these effects and makes them almost instantaneous, producing a short-lived burst of pleasurable sensation ('rush'). Injection under the skin or into the muscle gives a slower and less intense effect. Sniffing heroin also gives a slower and less intense effect than intravenous injection. When smoked, the effects of heroin can be expected to come on about as quickly as intravenous injection, but to be much less intense as the available dose is used over a period of time rather than injected all at once.

Long-term use

Tolerance develops to opiates such that someone in search of frequently repeated euphoria must increase the dose and/or change their method of administration. However, there comes a point when no further increases in dose can restore the positive effects of the drug and it is taken just to feel 'normal'. Intravenous injection maximises the effects of a given amount of heroin and produces a much more intense immediate experience, so as tolerance develops (and perhaps as money runs short) there may be a tendency to move from sniffing or smoking heroin to injection. Since tolerance also develops to the respiratory depressant effects of opiates, gradual escalation of dose does not in itself lead to risk of death through overdose. However, fatal overdoses can happen when opiate users take their usual dose after a break during which tolerance has faded.

After as little as several weeks on high, frequent doses, sudden withdrawal results in a variable degree of discomfort generally comparable to a bout of influenza. The effects start eight to 24 hours after the last 'fix' and include aches, tremor, sweating and chills, sneezing and yawning, muscular spasms. They generally fade in seven to ten days but feelings of weakness and loss of well-being last for several months. Abrupt opiate withdrawal is rarely life-threatening and is considerably less dangerous than withdrawal from alcohol.

Physical dependence is not as significant as the strong psychological dependence developed by some long-term users. Dependence of any kind is not inevitable and some people use heroin on an occasional basis. The physiological effects of long-term opiate use are rarely serious in themselves. They include respiratory complaints, constipation and menstrual irregularity. At higher doses chronic sedation can occur, but at moderate doses users can function normally. However, the consequences of injecting opiates and of a drug using lifestyle can be serious.

Among regular injectors, there is commonly physical damage associated with poor hygiene and the injection of adulterants. Adulterants contribute to respiratory disease, skin lesions, tetanus (with injection under the skin) and other complications depending on the agent used and the individual's sensitivity. Decreased appetite and apathy can contribute to disease caused by poor nutrition, self-neglect and bad housing. Repeated heroin sniffing may damage structures in the nose.

On the other hand, because opiates in themselves are relatively safe drugs, addicts in receipt of opiates on prescription and who maintain a stable, hygienic lifestyle, can be virtually indistinguishable from non-drug users, and suffer no serious physical damage. However as opiates are the most commonly injected drugs of misuse in Britain, those users who do inject face a high risk of becoming infected with the AIDS virus. Opiate use during pregnancy may result in smaller babies, who may suffer severe withdrawal symptoms after birth.

Mixing with other drugs

The combination of one drug on top of another on mind and body can produce complex effects, as yet little understood. As a general rule, it is probable that drugs of a similar nature and action upon the body, i.e. two stimulants or two depressants, will have an additive effect, resulting in greater stimulation or depression, depending on the drug types. Taking therefore, amphetamine on top of cocaine, will increase feelings of energy and activity, as well as paranoia, aggression and anxiety, not to mention a heavy drawn-out recovery period to contend with later.

Mixing drugs which bring on opposite effects, such as speed and heroin, or speed and alcohol, has more unpredictable consequences, depending on factors such as the user's mood, individual reaction to either drug, the order in which the drugs are taken, and how much of each is taken. Amphetamine taken while drunk, for example, may make one individual feel more awake and in control, or may make another feel more drunk and aggressive, exaggerating their drunken behaviour.

Combinations with hallucinogens are more complex still, with mood, situational circumstances and personality playing an even greater role in drug effects. Stimulants may add to the intensity of hallucinations or visual distortions, often prolonging the experience. Depressants on the other hand may lessen the degree of intensity, or may enhance feelings of confusion and bring on mood swings.

Taken from *Drug Abuse Briefing: A guide to the non-medical use of drugs in Britain (7th Edition, 1999)* produced by the Institute for the Study of Drug Dependence.

Please remember that there will be systems within your area for working with issues of substance use and misuse. These may include Drugs Action Teams, Community Alcohol Teams, Community Drugs Teams, Young Peoples Drugs Teams and a significant provision of help from voluntary groups and agencies. It is important to get to know how your local systems work and what help is available.

Appendix 2 Facts about Child Protection Systems in Britain

History

There has been substantial societal concern about child abuse in Britain for over one hundred and twenty years. The modern child protection system began in 1974 following the death, through abuse, of a child called Maria Colwell. The subsequent inquiry and report about Maria (DHSS, 1974) created a significant public and political demand for change in child protection processes. The government issued advice to local child care agencies to set up systems to recognise and deal with physical abuse and to ensure that staff from different agencies worked together more constructively.

The 1980s saw child protection systems in Britain become more concerned about the poor recognition of child sexual abuse. In Cleveland, in 1987, 165 children were diagnosed as having been sexually abused. In the inquiry that followed (Butler-Sloss, 1988) the child protection system in Cleveland was criticised for its handling of the children and parents concerned and the tabloid press criticised the system for its over-identification of abuse and over-intrusion into families.

The Cleveland report was to influence the direction of the new Children Act 1989 (see below) and encouraged the government to seek a new balance between protecting children and supporting parents. In 1988, 1991 and 1999 three *Working Together* documents were published to guide inter-agency co-operation in child protection work.

By the mid 1990s the government was still dissatisfied with the new balance that had been created by the Children Act 1989 and published a series of research reports concerning child protection systems (DoH, 1995). This research was critical of the number of children and families needlessly included in child protection systems that could more usefully have been dealt with using child in need/family support services. Many child protection systems began a process (refocusing) that held more children outside the child protection system and dealt with them as children in need.

Legislation and guidance

The legislation that currently underpins most child protection work is the Children Act 1989 (this act was significantly influenced by the UN charter on the rights of the child). The Act provides the framework for child protection work including sections on legal duties with regard to children (Parts ii, iv and v), but also it provides a legislative framework for working with children in need (Part iii). The Children Act was accompanied by a series of detailed guidances with more specific instruction on various aspects of child care and child protection.

The government also has published more practice guidance for staff via the Department of Health, the Home Office and the Department for Education and Employment. *Working Together to Safeguard Children* (December 1999) deals with inter-agency co-operation and organisation and the *Assessment Framework for Children in Need and their Families* (April 2000) proposes a new assessment framework for the measurement of the strengths and needs of children and families.

Local structures and systems

At a local level, the organisation that oversees child protection work is called the Area Child Protection Committee (ACPC). The ACPC is an umbrella organisation that includes senior representatives from health, social services, education, police, probation, the courts, the voluntary and non-statutory sectors, users representatives, representatives from ethnic minority communities and representatives from local armed forces.

It is the ACPC's role to co-ordinate child protection activity through local procedures, guidance, protocols, training and reviews. The child protection system in each local area (there are over 120 ACPCs in Britain) is different from all others, even though all are fed by the same national legislation and guidance.

The child protection process

Although local child protection processes vary, they all go through similar key stages when approaching a child who may have been abused. At most stages of the process the threshold for further progress is 'continuing significant harm'. It is important to remember that the system is designed to allow children and families to exit at any stage if continuing significant harm is thought unlikely.

Early stages: There are several early stages that a child might go through before entering the child protection system. The child may go through various 'child in need' processes, or be held within a single agency system if the level of concern is relatively low.

Referral: This is the process in which a practitioner or a member of the public notifies the local social services team that a child who lives in their area may be at risk of abuse (significant harm). This process may be problematic if there is a different threshold of concern between referrer and social work team.

Investigation/assessment: If the referral is accepted by the social work team they are obliged to undertake an investigation and an assessment of the child concerned. This process will involve gathering information from all relevant agencies, interviewing the referrer, the child, the child's siblings, the child's parents and anyone else with relevant information to offer. This investigation and assessment is to establish if there is the likelihood of continuing significant harm, if so, the child moves on to the next stage. For more serious cases of abuse and for most cases of child sexual abuse this investigation will frequently be shared between social services and special police teams (family support units).

Medical (if necessary): If the child has been the target for recent physical assault, severe neglect or sexual assault it is probable that the child will need a full medical examination. For neglect and physical assault the medical will usually be undertaken by a hospital paediatrician, for sexual assault the child will usually be examined by a police surgeon.

Child protection conference: The child protection conference is the most important formal event in the child protection process. The conference task is to weigh the likelihood and significance of ongoing significant harm, to decide whether to place the child's name on the child protection register and to establish the membership and focus of the new core group. The conference is also the starting point of future inter-agency working and future partnerships between child, family and practitioners. All relevant practitioners, adults with parental responsibility and (sometimes) the child will be included.

The conference goes through three stages:

1. The introduction stage where all present introduce themselves and explain their contact with the child and family.
2. The information sharing stage where all share their information about the strengths and deficits of child care within the family.
3. The decision-making stage where a decision is taken whether to place the child's name on the at-risk register, a key worker and a core group is nominated and the key parts of the child protection plan are outlined.

Core group: The core group is the vehicle that carries through the child protection plan of the conference. It is made up of between five and ten people, usually including parents, a social worker, a health visitor, an education representative and other key practitioners in the child or parent's lives. The core group's job is to undertake a full assessment, to oversee therapeutic work with the family and to continue to monitor and act upon the possibility of continuing significant harm.

Review conference: The review conference takes place within six months of the original conference. It is a gathering of relevant practitioners and the family to review the progress of the child protection plan and outline necessary changes to that plan. If sufficient progress has been achieved the child's name may be removed from the register.

Inter-agency working/role of the SSD

The child protection process is an inter-agency process where all agencies and practitioners who are involved with children and families pool their skills, knowledge and resources to better protect and support children. However, a leading role has been given, by government, to the SSD or more accurately the field social worker. The discussion between the inter-agency process and the key role of the social worker is a central debate in child protection systems and is worked out in different ways in different systems. Who cares for the child protection 'baby' and how that care is shared out is an ongoing discussion in most systems.

Please remember all child protection systems are different and have different ways of operating. It is important to find out which system you are part of and to discover what its particular procedures and processes are.